Praise for
Disconnect to Connect

"Through personal narrative and sound psychological science, Amy Vetter helps illuminate how the stories we often inhabit impact how we witness our experience of ourselves, others, and the world around us. Through understanding this impact, we can live more authentically and with greater compassion toward both ourselves and those we encounter along this journey. Her use of practical exercises at each chapter's end helps deepen our understanding of her teachings."

—Keith Bernardo, Ph.D., Clinical Psychologist

"Amy Vetter's *Disconnect to Connect* is overflowing with thoughtful insights on balancing 'business' with 'bliss'; this is particularly relevant in today's evolving professional services environment. Her personal story is truly inspiring, and her ability to bring awareness to her own vulnerability provides ample opportunities for the reader to reflect on ways to be more mindful and present in their own daily lives. I am a better person for having read Amy's book and aspire to implement many of Amy's best practices. Namaste."

—Michael Horowitz, Executive Director, BDO Alliance USA

"They say, 'We all have a story to tell,' and Amy is certainly no exception. Amy's vulnerability and courage to share is truly impressive. I was deeply moved by how she was able to face and overcome many challenges in her life. Rather than hiding her struggles she embraced them, showing us that even the greatest of obstacles can be overcome. The story of her journey has helped me unlock some of my own stories and given me insights that I had lost sight of. Additionally, her book has helped my youngest daughter by giving her perspective and inspiration as she navigates her own life's adventures. Amy has also included helpful insights from her podcast, *Breaking Beliefs*, making her book not only a powerful narrative, but a valuable guide to help each of us on our own journeys. I highly recommend her book to anyone looking for inspiration and encouragement on their own path."

—**Byron Patrick,** CPA, CITP, CGMA,
Vice President–Client Success, The B3 Method Institute

"Thank you, Amy Vetter, for sharing your stories and showing such vulnerability with your personal backstories! I am so grateful for the timing of the teachings you share in *Disconnect to Connect*. The depth of insight you provide is so well timed for many of us who are looking for a better way to inspire and impact others, especially during this new era—post-Covid—when we are all aiming and searching for a more humane way forward. Understanding and appreciating other colleagues' backstories and having the courage to share our own personal stories will open up opportunities and possibilities for a better way forward!"

—**Paul Peterson,** CEO, Wiss & Company, LLP

"This book made me reflect on the idea that everyone has a past and, even though those past events may have been painful to experience, they have all worked together to make you who you are today. I thank Amy for being willing to share her experience with others so we may realize that we are not alone—we are not broken—we can succeed in spite of the things that may have hurt us. Positive and negative influences all work together to guide our path and bring us to where we were meant to be . . . thank you for being willing to be vulnerable and share with others, so we might be able to make connections with those who will help us through our own journey."

—Melissa Harbert, MBA, Head of Markets & Consulting, Revecore

"*Disconnect to Connect* is essential reading for anyone ready to do the difficult work of overcoming recurring patterns that hinder progress—professional and personal. Amy's open approach to using her own raw life experience as a case study is effective and authentic, as she shows us the possibility of creating new belief systems to propel our lives in meaningful and satisfying directions."

—Brian Austin, Director, Public Relations, Avalara

"I can summarize this book in two words. Emotional Intelligence. So many organizations say they want to 'train' their people in emotional intelligence, yet this book proves the best way to attain it. Amy's openness and vulnerability throughout this book make me want to do the same. Others should follow along and use this book as a guide to become more self-aware and improve their own emotional intelligence. Well done."

—Mark Koziel, President & CEO, Allinial Global

"Amy invites you into an engaging reflection of her personal trials and challenges and what she has learned from them. These stories are punctuated by tools and exercises designed to help you harmonize both work and life's challenges into your own personal bliss. Her vulnerability is engaging and pulls you in. Thought-provoking and interesting throughout, *Disconnect to Connect* gives valuable takeaways you can immediately apply to your own life."

—**Ryan Schaffer,** CFO, Expensify

"*Disconnect to Connect* is an invigorating approach to identifying and overcoming barriers we are often unaware of. This book is relatable, insightful, and refreshingly transparent in a world that could use more of this. This journey will allow you to tap into your desired purpose and talents in a new and powerful way."

—**Angie Grissom, MBA,** Owner and Chief Relationship Officer, The Rainmaker Companies

"Amy Vetter blends the perfect combination of business and tech acumen with personal growth advice. She is unfiltered in sharing her own experiences in her writing and keynotes, making her relatable to any audience. Amy's the business yogi we all need!"

—**Kacee Johnson,** Top 25 Thought Leader, Top 100 Most Influential, Most Powerful Women in Accounting

"If you want to believe that there is a chance at healing and living a whole life despite a traumatic childhood, this book is for you. Amy's book takes us on a profoundly authentic pilgrimage, sharing her journey and a treasurable internal dialog that's so familiar and not spoken out loud enough. This book provides a blueprint for a healing journey, the courage to go on the path, and an account that won't leave you feeling lonely. Read this book . . . and reinvigorate your life!"

—**Bharat Nain,** Co-Organizer, TEDxChelseaPark

"Wow! Amy Vetter's *Disconnect to Connect* is a powerful, vulnerable story illustrating the tremendous influence our formative life stories have on how we behave and think. Amy's straightforward telling of her own life story and journey to free herself from historical conditioning and habits is unvarnished. Her courageous search for understanding, meaning, independence, and acceptance is inspiring, and her practical and actionable ideas at the end of each chapter make the same search available to us all."

—**Jennifer Lee-Wilson,** Cofounder and Partner, Convergence Coaching, LLC

"Just as I have been so lucky to receive all my life from my mother, this book is a mix of life, career, family, and relationship advice that will allow you to take a new perspective and leave a better person. Her teachings continued in my reading of this book. Like me, you may find yourself reflecting in ways you haven't before, or you may be able to discover something about yourself you didn't know before. I know I did . . . once again."

—**Jagger Vetter,** Amy's son (22-year-old environmental engineering/ MBA student at the University of Cincinnati)

"It's beyond amazing seeing my mom's inspiring story finally being released after years of her persevering through setbacks. I've had the fortune of being raised and taught by the strong, courageous person you'll learn about in this book, and I'm so excited for her grit to be displayed to the world."

—**Austin Vetter,** Amy's son (18-year-old senior high school student)

DISCONNECT
TO
CONNECT

TAP INTO THE POWER WITHIN YOU
TO CREATE THE LIFE YOU DESIRE

AMY VETTER

RIVER GROVE
BOOKS

Published by River Grove Books
Austin, TX
www.rivergrovebooks.com

Distributed by River Grove Books

Design and composition by Greenleaf Book Group and Sheila Parr
Cover design by Greenleaf Book Group and Sheila Parr
Cover images used under license from © iStockphoto/kaisorn and © iStockphoto/valio84sl

Publisher's Cataloging-in-Publication data is available.

Print ISBN: 978-1-63299-679-4

eBook ISBN: 978-1-63299-680-0

First Edition

To my sons, Jagger and Austin.
My life—and my journey—is dedicated to the both of you.

Contents

AUTHOR'S NOTE

A Letter to Readers

Thank you for choosing to go on this journey with me. Before we begin, I want to share why I wrote this book, so you can put it into perspective as you read the stories and lessons.

I began to see a therapist when I was 32 years old. At the time, I had no idea how many layers I had built up inside to avoid the pain I carried. I was aware that I felt off, but I didn't know why. However, once I began the process, the layers were gradually peeled off. I had to step back and view my life from a different perspective. During my therapy, I was going almost three hours at a time every week to make sense of what felt like mud. I felt stuck, but there was no way around it, so I had to keep going if I was going to make a change for myself.

Once I got to the other side of this intense therapy, my therapist suggested that I write a book and share these stories. He felt that too many people struggle with similar stories in their life and do not realize how others work through them.

We don't always realize how others are doing internally because that is not what they expose to the world. We've been taught to show up with a smile and keep everything inside. But this ends up leaving us stuck and unable to help our friends, families, and work colleagues in the way we need to in order to make it a productive day.

For 13 years, I made notes of my stories in hopes that I could share them one day. It has taken that long to find the courage to bring this book to life. Some of these stories I share are hard to relive, but they may unlock your own internal stories.

I have tried to be as vulnerable as possible in this book and share what I feel will help others. Although some details are omitted for privacy purposes, these stories I am sharing are to help you identify and unlock the stories of your own that you may be holding inside. It's possible that, like me, maybe you didn't realize what has been a barrier in your own work or personal life.

These stories I share about myself are designed to help you brainstorm your own stories as you read them, and to use them to aid in your own growth. In turn, hopefully, you will realize you are not alone and it is possible to find your own path to recovery and growth.

I am not a therapist. These are my own perspectives, research, and learnings I have found along my life journey. My choices are my own. They are not for everyone, and they have been very hard. It's up to you to determine your own path to healing, find the solutions that work best for you, and don't put a timeline on them. No one can measure pain or trauma, compare one person's experience to another's, and make sound judgments about whether one is worse than another. We all experience things differently, and we need to honor what we feel and not compare ourselves to someone else. Each person matters. You matter.

Take what I share as a brainstorming exercise and choose how it relates to you—or not. If a story or lesson doesn't resonate, then let it go. If you feel off or need someone to talk to, it's wise to hire a therapist. If the stories here unlock your own, speaking with an independent third party and medical professional is the responsible decision.

Each of our journeys is unique, so understand that while I provide some methods to heal from my own experiences and research, they may not always work for you, and you may find your own strategies that resonate better.

Awareness is the true gift I have received from my path. I am now aware of how I feel internally and can analyze it and then decide how to respond. There is no quick fix. And life happens. So, we may figure one thing out, then get another unexpected twist along the way, and have to pause, pivot, and decide how to respond again.

Also, these stories are from my own perspective, perception, and interpretation. They are about how my experiences affected my life and the people around me. What is true in life is that each person has their own version of the same story. Everyone I mention may or may not agree with my perspective. However, these stories are from my vantage point and are what I alone experienced.

When we are children, we have limited perspective that would allow us to recognize that something is wrong. The only reality we know is what has occurred in that brief time frame. We may feel stressed internally or display outward behaviors that show we unconsciously know something is wrong. However, as adults, we have the opportunity, if we choose, to review our past and have a different perspective with more life experience under our belt.

I realized during therapy that even though I was an adult, I still thought of memories from a 16-year-old's viewpoint rather than from the perspective of an adult woman, mother, and professional. Once I began a career and started a family, I saw everything differently. I realized that the reality I had known didn't feel right anymore.

When we notice this, it's our choice to allow it to surface, decipher it, and then decide how it will affect our future. Rather than letting the past control us, we have the power to create change in our lives. The hard choices come along because we can no longer pretend that we don't understand the need to change.

We choose whether we disconnect from our internal stories, behaviors, patterns, and habits and decide instead to connect to this new awareness to continue to grow, to better ourselves and those around us, with no excuses or blame, just love.

INTRODUCTION

A Brief History

We all have our stories. We often can use those back-stories as the reason we react to different situations the way we do. I have found in my life that stories have been used by my family members as their reason for why they behaved in a certain way toward me or someone else rather than taking personal responsibility for how they affected the people around them. Those stories that were told to me began with stories of my grandparents.

My grandma from Minnesota was supposedly one of the most beautiful women in her community. At least, that's what I heard from my mom and her friends. At my grandma's funeral, I remember how many people made a point to tell me what a beauty she was. From as long as I can remember, it is also what my mom never stopped talking about.

My grandma was a Russian immigrant and didn't marry until her late 30s, and later divorced in her 40s, which was uncommon at the time. Once my grandparents divorced, my mom told me that my grandma favored my uncle, and my grandfather preferred my mom. From the stories I have been told, I made my own assumption that my grandma felt jealous of my mom's relationship with my grandfather.

The one thing that both my grandparents agreed upon was how proud they were of my mom's talent for playing the piano. As a child, she practiced a minimum of three hours a day. She won state championships for the piano multiple times and soloed with the Minneapolis Symphony Orchestra as a teenager.

As a little girl, some of my most poignant memories were the few times my mom sat down at the piano and played. I would lie on the carpeted floor, close my eyes, and let the music fill me. When I opened my eyes, I watched my mom's body fully get into the music and sway to the softness or loudness of the music. To this day, I tear up when I hear the piano piece "*Clair de Lune,*" as I remember her playing it with such passion and feeling.

My mom's relationship with my grandma was full of turmoil. There was a significant focus on being beautiful rather than on talent. My mom believed that my grandma never thought that she, her daughter, was attractive enough. My grandma put my mom in multiple beauty pageants, and, because of my mom's piano talent and good looks, she often did well in these competitions.

My grandma had my mom stay home from school on a few sunny days so she could suntan, because, according to my grandma, she looked prettier with a tan. My grandma even put a timer outside so my mom could flip over at regular intervals to even her tan.

Because of her own negative experiences when she was young, my mom reinforced that I should never rely on my appearance. She didn't allow me to do the "girl" activities like cheerleading and dance that I asked to do, because in her mind, you were celebrating someone else's accomplishments and not your own, or she felt I wouldn't be naturally good enough.

By the time my mom went to college, she and my grandma were no longer on speaking terms because my mom was the unlucky one who answered the phone when my grandma's brother called one morning.

Apparently, my grandma was angry with her brother and wasn't speaking to him at the time. However, on that particular morning he was driving to California to visit his first grandchild and had called my grandma so he could say goodbye and tell her he loved her.

My mom answered the phone and asked my grandma to speak to him but my grandma refused.

He told my mom to let my grandma know he loved her and then he left for California. Tragically, my grandma's brother and his wife were killed in a car accident on their way to visit their daughter's new family.

My grandma was never the same, and she never forgave my mom for being the last one to talk with him. With this experience and the double whammy of my mom being my grandfather's favorite, their relationship didn't have much of a chance.

When my mom went to college, she and my grandma would pass each other in the house and never speak. My mom eventually moved into her sorority house on campus so she could have a place where she felt she belonged.

One of my strongest memories of their strained relationship was when my grandma was dying. I was in eighth grade. I remember being alone with my grandma in the hospital lobby while waiting for my mom to come from the parking lot. My grandma looked at me, then through the windows, where she watched with disgust as my mother walked in. My grandma turned to me and said, "You think your mom is *soooo* special, don't you?"

I answered: "Yes, I do."

Then my grandma turned her head in disappointment.

At that moment, I felt proud that I had defended my mom, even though I loved my grandma and didn't want to disappoint her.

I also have memories of how messy my grandma was. She never put away her clothes and many mornings did not bother doing her hair or makeup. When she did apply makeup, it was often crooked and messed up because her hands and face trembled from a disease she had contracted as a child. Her nails were usually dirty from the hours she spent gardening.

But she didn't care. She saw herself as beautiful up until her last breath.

I had seen pictures of my grandma when she was younger, and she was a glamorous-looking woman. But I never saw her beauty from the same vantage point as my mom did, who had to live up to her "legend" beauty status. Maybe it was because I saw her being mean to my mom and I was protective. I didn't understand the hype, nor the pressure, to look like her. I thought my mom was one of the most beautiful women I knew, so I was constantly trying to see why Mom thought she wasn't as attractive as my grandma. But I never truly understood.

This relationship between my grandma and my mom had an immense impact on my mom, not only in the way she placed importance on beauty for herself and those around her, but also because my grandma was so unkempt, my mom ended up the complete opposite. She tried to control life by being hyper-focused on cleanliness and planning out every minute of the day. As my mom aged, this became a stronger trait, and if you deviated from the way she wanted things, you would quickly see you were disappointing her.

From the time I was 12, I was responsible for cleaning my parents' bedroom and bathroom. My mom always inspected my work when I was finished. She would point out what I missed and what I needed to redo. If she caught a smear on the mirror, or I forgot to clean something in the grout between the bathroom tiles, I had to start all over.

Then there was my dad's side and his mom—my grandma from Arizona—who created trauma for my father. She was not a part of my life, as I only met her once. From everything I have heard about her, she apparently was an awful person. She was so bad that when my parents were preparing to marry, their family doctor privately gave both of them Valium to survive her wrath so they could get through their wedding.

I was told she even made my mom's father (my grandfather) cry once because she was so mean to him. When my mom was first married to my father, she couldn't get an appointment for any local beauty salons once she told them her new married last

name. That name was on a list of clients they would not do business with. (My mom had to sneak in using her maiden name.)

My most vivid memory of my paternal grandmother is when
my parents were in divorce proceedings when I was 16. She called
me one day after school. I picked up the phone, and all she said
was, "You ask your mom how it feels to know that you and your
brothers are no longer in my will." And then she hung up.

My parents met in college on a blind date. By both of their
accounts, it was the first time they had another person in their life
who cared about them and truly loved them. I believe they were
happy together for many years.

However, my brothers and I never had parents who were
whole from an emotional perspective and ready to be selfless
because they had never worked on the trauma they endured with
their parents. Our parents could not put us before their own
emotional needs and the internal demons they suffered because
of their parents.

I loved my parents very much, and they were my entire
focus, even above myself, when I was growing up. I wanted
them to be happy, and I didn't want them to suffer from their
past experiences.

THE NEED TO UNDERSTAND
OUR INTERNAL STORIES

You may be wondering: How did I know all of my parents'
backstories?

Because I was the confidant to both of my parents from
an early age, they shared their stories with me and, eventually,

their feelings about each other. At the time, I felt fortunate to be the child who knew everything. I know now that I knew too much, and it shaped me as a person. I felt responsible for them and needed to be their protector. Each would be jealous of my relationship with the other and wanted reassurance that I was closer to one or the other as I grew older.

Even when their behavior was terrible toward me, I gave them excuses. I held the "honor" of knowing their past stories. It was my responsibility not to take their treatment of me personally and protect them instead of myself.

As we become adults, these internal stories create the excuses we use for our own behavior when we act inappropriately. This behavior can range from minor things we do each day to more significant issues that show up in our lives. From the work I have done personally—as well as accounts from others I have either known or read about—I've learned that we each have the power to break the patterns from past generations and choose to design the future we desire.

Beyond bringing these internal stories and habits into our personal lives, we can often carry them unintentionally into the workplace. In times of change, whether in our personal or business lives, we can feel alone and create unnecessary fear based on our past stories, rather than stepping back and creating space for how we think and how to intentionally move forward positively.

And that is the purpose of this book—to share stories of my own journey and those of others, as well as research I have found along the way—to help you uncover your own stories. By doing this work, it can not only help us to become better individuals at home and personally, but also benefit our leadership abilities in the workplace and help us become a better colleague to others.

In the business world, I have seen leaders spend more time focusing on change management and the future of work instead of creating stronger human connections to ensure everyone knows they are supported and not alone during the change process.

This is the goal of being what I call a "Connected Leader." A Connected Leader has authentic compassion and empathy for the people around them and creates a safe, nurturing environment so each person can be at their best. This allows people to show up as they are and have the support they need to improve themselves and observe the patterns and habits that may be holding them back, based on their past stories.

By doing the work to understand what drives our own behaviors, we are better able to lead others with compassion.

My first interaction with a Connected Leader occurred when I was in junior high and played violin. I often felt alone and nervous when I was preparing for an upcoming orchestra audition. I questioned my ability to do well and felt vulnerable, anticipating going before the judges. In those moments, my violin teacher would say in his Russian accent, "If you're no good, I'm no good. That's the way 'tis." This assured me that I wasn't alone, and we were a team. He met me where I was at, understood my fear, and walked alongside me so I could achieve the outcome I wanted.

Over the years consulting with business professionals, I have found that what gets in the way of progress and change management is not necessarily learning new business processes or technology. Rather, people's individual patterns and internal stories get stuck in their heads, which drives the fear of the unknown. This fear causes people to doubt their ability to excel in an evolving environment and as a result, they resist making the necessary changes.

We often forget that each person carries their own internalized stories throughout the day. When we realize this as leaders or co-workers, we can be more mindful about how we show up, take responsibility, and pivot to nurture the people around us so no one feels alone.

As Connected Leaders, we can make a choice to create a safe and nurturing environment and a supportive culture to embrace opportunities, one employee at a time, that not only benefits the business but also creates more fulfillment in our jobs and builds stronger human connections, whether at home or in the workplace.

It's up to us whether we choose to take the journey and create more awareness of ourselves, so we can continue to learn and grow and be intentional about the future we want to make for ourselves and those around us.

This book aims to show you the power of creating your own belief systems rather than allowing your internal backstories to create them. By sharing my journey of how I discovered my voice for telling my story, and relaying the advice and wisdom from other luminaries in the business and wellness worlds who have traveled the same path, I describe methods I've used to show me when I am off internally, rather than blaming circumstances outside of my control.

This journey is about awareness, discovering a better understanding of where we came from, who we are, and best of all, using that awareness to transform into the person we want to be.

At the end of each chapter, I have included the following:

- A "B³ Break" box that provides a reminder of how to apply my Business, Balance, and Bliss approach by practicing some of the tools or exercises I provide in each chapter. You have the option to make notes and record your thoughts in real time at the end of each chapter about how you may implement new practices or approaches for yourself or people around you from the stories and research you read.

- A *Breaking Beliefs* Podcast Spotlight." This segment features advice from business leaders and wellness experts that I've interviewed on my podcast. These excerpts come from full interviews on the podcast with links to the entire conversation if you want to hear more about their story.

- A recap of the main points, which I call "Mindful Moments." Take some time to pause and consider these lessons before you move to the next chapter. Ask yourself the following:

  - How can I incorporate one or more of these ideas into my life?

  - What kind of support from possible outside experts such as therapists, business coaches, friends, family, and other trusted advisors could help me navigate and practice this?

- Which of the suggestions can help me disconnect so I can reconnect to myself and the people around me in a positive way to create the energy and life I desire?

We all play a part in others' lives in some way—as sons and daughters, brothers and sisters, mothers and fathers, spouses, business leaders, friends, co-workers, and citizens. We have so many roles to play. But how well we do that begins with knowing ourselves so we can be there for others. And that begins with uncovering our stories.

CHAPTER 1

Our Backstories

"Be careful of thinking you know a person so well. Like comic books,
everyone has an origin story . . . and oftentimes it ain't pretty."

—H. L. SUDLER

Everyone has a backstory. We interact with people daily through business, friendships, family, and acquaintances. But how much do we really know their stories? You may think you know someone or know them well enough to understand them, but do you really?

The problem is that we don't fully understand others because, in essence, we don't necessarily take the time to get to know ourselves enough. Do we really understand what created our own stories and belief systems that we walk around with each day? How did we become the person we see in the mirror and the world interacts with? I'm talking about our strengths, weaknesses, assets, and flaws—everything that makes us unique.

Being aware of who we truly are takes constant work. It's tough to be honest with ourselves and take a raw, unfiltered look at what got us to this moment and why. It takes courage to do this deep work and allow ourselves to be aware, conscious, and feel our existence.

But this kind of honest reflection will do wonders for how you decide to present yourself to the world, and perhaps most important, how you interact with others. In the past, you may have reacted in the moment to someone's comment or behavior. However, through this new approach to vulnerability you may now have more compassion for each person's journey and be able to become present in who you are while realizing that each person is walking their own unique path as well.

Understanding our backstories and how in essence they create our everyday behavioral patterns can provide the wisdom we need to be better business leaders as well as better friends, spouses, and people in general.

My goal here is to provide examples using stories of my own from the continuous work I do now and have done along my journey to break through my own patterns. This is with the hope that you are able to tap into your own stories. As you read along, I want you to think about what comes up for you and utilize the resources I provide, as well as finding your own that can help. The intention is to provide a path for you to become more aware of the patterns that may be holding you back from your next best opportunity or relationship, or even preventing you from finding peace within.

LOSING AND FINDING MY VOICE

At times, I dread sleeping because I have a recurring experience when I dream.

I am being attacked, and I try to scream so someone will hear me, but there is no sound that comes out of my mouth when I try. Or I am trying to tell a family member something that upsets me. But no words come out. I strain to say something, anything, but all I can manage is a faint whisper because my throat closes, I am straining to speak, and I can barely breathe.

I often shake myself to wake up out of this nightmare, out of breath, my heart racing.

It took me years to realize that this dream about no one hearing my voice or noticing me was based on reality.

For as long as I can remember, I felt no one was truly hearing me. Not in the sense of hearing my words, but not caring what I needed, so they didn't listen to my words.

What I came to realize once I made some healthy changes in my life is that the dream represented my backstories of traumatic experiences in my family that I carried in my body and mind without realizing it. Throughout my life, my need to be heard from a place of empathy and compassion was often unmet by the people I trusted and loved the most.

As I grew up, to the outside world, my family looked perfect. Both my parents were college-educated and successful in their fields. My mom owned a commercial and residential cleaning business with locations in three cities. My father was a professor and an avid weightlifter in his free time. I had two talented brothers who played sports, music, and were artistic. I played violin and viola, painted, and was a competitive swimmer. My father coached our soccer teams as we grew up. We lived in a typical Midwestern, upper-middle-class neighborhood complete with a cul-de-sac, and we had a big backyard for playing with our friends on our street.

What people didn't see was what was happening inside the house. My parents both had a history of emotionally abusive families, and probably without them even realizing it, they carried that pattern of behavior to the next generation.

One of my brothers spent most of his time in his room, keeping himself away from my father starting at a young age. Alternatively, I witnessed my other brother working hard to be noticed and loved without earning the affection he desired. As the oldest child, I spent my time being the protector and caretaker for each person, trying to keep the peace and wanting everyone to be happy and feel loved. However, in reality the truth was that I found it difficult to please them and get the love I needed in return, no matter how hard I tried.

My mother opened her business when I was in second grade. Prior to that, she was home with us. Her business had three locations, which took her out of town a lot. When she was in town, she worked late hours at the office, not having the technology we do today to work remotely. Often, by the time she got home we were already asleep.

As the years went by, my father grew more frustrated and stressed as her schedule became more demanding, and many times the result was my brothers and I bore the brunt of how he was feeling. By middle school, many of the household responsibilities fell on my shoulders. I had to grow up fast to take care of everything around the house and what my brothers needed as well. My father's anger got worse over the years, and sometimes he got physical with my brothers and me. However, both parents contributed to the emotional scars we carried as children, as emotions escalated and tension increased between my parents.

By the time I was 16 years old, my mother had lost her business. My parents got divorced, the credit cards were maxed out, and we lost our house. I was put in charge of answering the phone when creditors called for my parents.

At the time, the technology for caller ID didn't exist, so there was no way to know whether or not you should pick up the phone. My responsibility was to tell any creditor that my parents were not available and take a message. Because of the credit problems, we also had to hold a sale to sell everything in the house. I watched as strangers walked into each room of our house and decided to purchase my bedroom set and other old cherished toys, jewelry, and clothing I had. I remember hiding a few items that I kept after my grandma in Minnesota passed away so no one would buy them. Many tried to negotiate a lower price on our items because to them it was just a transaction and a great "find." I quickly found that my "things" were not of the same value to strangers as they were to me personally.

Once my parents were divorced, and the house was sold, my mom, brothers, and I moved to a town house. My brother, who was 13 at the time, and I, age 16, got multiple hourly jobs to help cover our family's daily expenses and put food on the table. I began working three jobs to get enough hours so that I could continue to play my viola and pay for viola lessons, buy clothes, and be able to participate in activities with my friends.

At one point, our financial situation got so bad that we didn't have enough money for groceries. My mom asked me to call my dad for help rather than her calling him herself. So I put aside my pride and begged my dad to help. He was less than sympathetic and left a single bag of groceries at the front door for the four of us. The despair I felt at that moment was immense as I watched out my window while he drove away. In turn, I tore down every picture I had on my wall and removed any pictures in my scrapbook of him and me. I neatly put them together in a box hidden away so I no longer would have the pain of looking at them and feel the disappointment of not being cared for. I can look back now and realize I didn't feel seen or heard by either parent. I hadn't found my voice yet.

FAMILY AFFAIRS

My parents' divorcing kicked off years of emotional turmoil for us all. It began one morning before school while my brother and I were eating breakfast at the kitchen table. My mom came in and sat down and announced that she would ask my dad for a divorce when he woke up. However, she told us that before she was going to say anything to him, she wanted us to confirm that this is what my brother and I wanted. We both agreed she should proceed.

By this age, my brother and I had experienced years of emotional and physical abuse from my father, and with my mother being away at work all the time, we were left to fend for ourselves with him. By this point, we were emotionally and mentally exhausted and relieved to have this decision made.

However, what my brother and I didn't know at the time was that my mom went in after that discussion with us to wake my dad up. She sat down on the bed, and her first words to him were that she *and* the kids wanted him to leave. That set off my father's anger, initiating a family war, not just against my mom, but against my brothers and me as well, for "teaming up" with her.

My dad allowed us to suffer financially as payback. He had a salaried job and could have chosen to help during some of those darkest days. But he didn't. It was what "we" deserved for kicking him out.

When it was time to go to court, my mom convinced me to testify against my dad. I was to tell the court that if they didn't make him financially support us, he wouldn't do it. With every fiber in me, I did not want to do this. I was sick to my stomach. But I wanted to show my mom and my brothers my loyalty, so I said I would. She convinced me that I was the only hope.

On the day of the hearing, she told me to braid my hair in pigtails and wear a skirt that went down to my calves. I never dressed like this, but she said it was necessary to look like an innocent child and not a complaining teenager.

Before the hearing, we met the attorney for breakfast. He put extra pressure on me about how I needed to answer questions and behave. I was getting more stressed out by the second. While I waited to testify, I kept going outside to get air and soon became sick in the bathroom. One of my mom's friends came that day to the hearing to support my mom. She found me in the bathroom. She told me I was doing the right thing and I was a good daughter.

When it was time to testify, I sat right across from my dad. I am sure it couldn't have been easy for him to have me on the stand. However, I was there for a reason, and he was making sure to hurt me so I could feel his pain. During the hearing, I felt like a tennis ball being volleyed over the net between my parents and their attorney.

Each time one of their lawyers asked me questions, I could feel the BAM! of being hit by their racquet. As I was asked questions, I watched my dad hand notes to his lawyer with his own questions to ask to make it harder on me.

All I ever wanted was for my family to be together and everyone to love each other. The love I felt filled me from my head to my toes. But each person in my family became more entrenched in their own perspective of the story over time, rather than wanting to care for one another and heal.

The anger and hurt feelings tore our family apart. Our parents cared more about their own feelings and "being right" than making sure my brothers and I were whole. The trauma didn't serve my brothers and me well, as we each suffered differently, but not together.

For a brief moment, after my father moved out, our house was peaceful. However, the trauma began to come out in ways we never could have predicted. My older brother ran away a month before he was supposed to graduate high school. He left a note for my mom that said something to the effect that the tide had come, and it was his time to leave.

It was frightening to not know where my brother had gone and if he was okay. My younger brother was increasingly sadder by the day, with both my father and brother gone. Once, he put his hand up when he was around nine years old, showing all five fingers, and said that "first we were five," then lowered his next finger, "then we were four," then dropped another, "and now we are three."

A few months later, we did find my runaway brother. When he came home, he announced that his baby was due in a few months. My brother's daughter ended up being one of the best things that ever happened to him—and me. A year later, he enlisted in the Army to take better financial care of her, and a few years after that, he was deployed to Iraq.

My other brother desperately wanted to live with my father as he grew older. He craved my father's approval and wanted him to love him so badly. When my younger brother was a teenager, my father agreed to take him, so "then we were two."

It was painful to watch both my brothers leave. I thought that even with all our shared trauma, my brothers and I would always have one another. But it didn't turn out that way. I was alone. As I learned along the way while growing up, there was no option to wallow. I shut down my insides and focused on my future. I worked each day to get myself out of this situation and create a new life for myself.

When people see me or my social media profiles and TEDx Talk video, they assume that everything just comes easy for me. But most of us don't know each other's backstories and how we got to where we are today.

For me, what's not exposed on my public profiles are the years of working multiple jobs simultaneously through high school and college from being a restaurant hostess, server, lifeguard, swim instructor, retail associate, and even a water aerobics instructor, to name a few. I did everything I could to keep up with my expenses from my teenage years through college.

Prior to all this I was a swimmer and played viola in a few orchestras. When the divorce happened, I had to give up the swim team in high school because there simply wasn't any time between being responsible for my brothers and taking them where they needed to go, as well as the housework I needed to do each day. I barely kept up my viola playing. It was nearly impossible for me to pay for private lessons and fit in orchestra rehearsals. When I was in college, I didn't live on campus because I couldn't afford it and needed to work, so I missed many experiences that most kids have.

Each day in college was work, classes, homework, and more work. During this time, I would envision what it would be like when I got through college and could better support myself and control the responsibilities in my life. It helped me to stay focused on my future rather than be sad about my current situation.

A LOOK AT BACKSTORIES

Looking back at my early life, I can see how these stories transformed me into the person I've become. Of course, my stories since then continue to evolve as I continue to grow.

I often think about how telling our stories—to ourselves and each other—can be transformative. But I've also always been curious about how our backstories can influence our belief systems and affect our interactions with those around us. We eventually know our own stories, but what about the people we work with and develop professional and personal relationships with? Do we really understand their backstories and what they carry internally?

What can we learn from them?

If my social media profiles had my complete backstory, would that change people's perceptions of me? Would it affect how they interact with me? Would they find more compassion when communicating with me?

Every day, we make assumptions about our co-workers or people we meet based on their outward appearance or how they behave. No matter who we are—at the lowest or highest levels of the organization—we are all guilty of it at one time or another.

If you knew the backstories of the people you work with, would you be more empathetic as you go through hard conversations at work? Would it affect your perspective on why they do what they do? How could this information help you arrive at a place of compromise rather than continuing to battle daily with a co-worker, customer, or employee?

When we go through change, we often don't observe why we believe what we do or what is holding us back. Are these beliefs our own—or what we were told to think growing up? These learned behaviors from childhood create the patterns we bring into adulthood.

Years ago, I spoke to a large conference audience. As I spoke, I got flashes of memories of my family and my past. At one point, for a split second, I felt vulnerable because no one knew that part of me. The self-talk began and I wondered:

- What if this audience knew I saw a therapist?

- What if they knew my family members didn't get along or didn't speak to one another?
- Would they still respect me or think I was worthy of speaking on this stage?

I had to quickly get myself to snap out of it, or I would have had a breakdown in front of everyone.

I felt shame. I inherently knew that I had earned the right to be on that stage. But nonetheless, I believed that the audience wouldn't respect me if they knew my whole story, the whole me.

Alternatively, I have learned that some of us may believe the opposite. We believe our life is not as hard as someone else's, so we do not have the right to share our pain. But there is no way to measure other people's pain. We all live our own experiences and can't compare the intensity of one person's suffering to another's.

I've also learned that it's not our job to protect other people's behavior. Everyone is responsible for their own actions. We each have our own story with different perspectives. We have a right to how we feel, without another person imposing their guidelines around it.

When we realize the effect of each person's behavior on us, we know it's our own story we need to decipher to create a deeper understanding. To improve how we show up in our lives, we need to acknowledge what is going on internally to better interact with the surrounding world.

Brené Brown, in her book *Daring Greatly: How the Courage to Be Vulnerable Transforms the Way We Live, Love, Parent, and Lead*, discusses how shame can create the fear that holds us back, rather than trying to push past it.[1] If, instead, we taught ourselves how to hold space for each person's story and were more understanding toward others, what power could we create with the people we work with? At home?

You can break those patterns. But it takes work. I spent years in therapy and went through my own self-discovery with coaches, learning yoga and its philosophy, going on retreats, and reading books. I also learned from people who appeared to have healthier family relationships, and I sought to model my own relationships after them.

Sometimes, taking a closer look at the conversations you have with yourself can eliminate self-doubt so you can begin the process of drafting your backstory. (To learn more about how to do this, see the *Breaking Beliefs* Podcast Spotlight: "Pillow Talk: Creating Awareness of the Self-Doubt to Get to the Truth," highlighted at the end of this chapter.[2])

And the work never stops. There continue to be self-discoveries every day; even when I think one issue for me is solved, another can arise. I have learned that there is no finish line. But what I am better at is awareness when I feel "off" internally. When my outside environment sends me signs that I am not showing up in the way I intend to, I know it's time to step back and pause,

---

1 New York: Penguin/Avery, 2012.

2 All excerpts here and in the following chapters can be found at my weekly podcast, *Breaking Beliefs*: https://www.amyvetter.com/breakingbeliefspodcast. Here you'll find interviews with leaders in an array of different professions. Each guest describes their own journey of breaking from what someone told them to believe or a belief they created on their own that wasn't serving them. They often share a similar message: To make positive change, it's a matter of taking full responsibility for our experiences and how we affect others around us and being open to seeking feedback.

observe, and better understand what I need to do to feel better for myself and create the energy I want for those around me.

Many of us make a choice to live out the journey that those before us never did. We do this by breaking through fear, belief systems, or other inherited tendencies, to enable us to live our dreams instead of choosing to continue the patterns before us.

By taking part in this journey, and with time and dedication, you too can cultivate the awareness to disconnect from your daily pressures. This can help you gain perspective on the patterns or internal stories that hold you back at work, in your personal life, or in future business roles.

This journey allows you to better connect to the power within you to design the life you desire. And it begins with your own stories.

B³ BREAK

What drives you in your work and career? And are you on the right path to reach your goals? Here is a checklist that can help you answer these questions and help you make the adjustments you need to succeed.

Aligning Your Inner Self to Your Work
(based on a personal checklist created by Kaye Ramos)

PURPOSE: To identify what drives you internally and align it to the work you do, rather than doing what you do because of what others want or have pressured you to do. By understanding your deep-rooted "why" based on your talents, strengths, experiences, and abilities, you will shift your focus to the bigger picture each day and be more fulfilled internally by the work you do, rather than looking for outside rewards.

INSTRUCTIONS: The following checklist provides you with a way to reflect internally. It's important to answer these questions on your work honestly, rather than how you would perceive others would want you to answer. There are only two options to choose from for each question—YES or NO. Tally your answers at the end and reflect on the result to determine what adjustments you would like to make in your life, or not.

Part 1: Your Performance Based on Your INNER Drive

TASK, ACTIVITY, or WORK I am performing right now:

_____

_____

I. Performance

I have nearly perfect performance when executing this task	YES	NO
I still feel motivated despite the number of years I have been doing this task	YES	NO
I see myself doing this task for years to come	YES	NO
I succeed most of the time when perform-ing this task	YES	NO
I lose account of the time when performing this task	YES	NO
I normally find myself finishing what I begin when doing this task	YES	NO
TOTAL PERFORMANCE	_____	

continued

II. Learning/Improvement

I am willing to engage in further learning like seminars or coaching to enhance my skills	YES	NO
I enjoy reading books, watching videos, or listening to audiobooks related to this task	YES	NO
I am willing to seek out new opportunities to exercise my strength on this task	YES	NO
I show an intrinsic motivation to do this task	YES	NO

TOTAL LEARNING / IMPROVEMENT   _____

III. Interpersonal

I engage with others who are knowledgeable about this task	YES	NO
I have or will receive recognition, awards, or praise for performing well on this task	YES	NO
People seek my help, advice, or support on this task	YES	NO
People approach me to do this task, even if outside my day job, for pay or charity	YES	NO

TOTAL INTERPERSONAL   _____

IV. Attitudes

I am optimistic despite failures when I perform this task	YES	NO
My creative juices flow on this task	YES	NO

I see myself continuing to perform this task in my career	YES	NO
I have had positive experiences when performing this task	YES	NO
I generate the best ideas on topics related to this task	YES	NO
I feel happy when I take actions on this task	YES	NO
I experience the best concentration when working on this task	YES	NO
TOTAL ATTITUDE	————	

V. Feelings

I find it easy to take actions and grab opportunities to use my strengths in this task	YES	NO
Without money, I am willing to embrace this task for years	YES	NO
I feel strong, enthusiastic, and powerful when I do this task	YES	NO
I feel frustrated, drained, or pressured when I do this task	YES	NO
I feel I was born with innate talents to execute this task	YES	NO
I feel I am my best self when doing this task	YES	NO
TOTAL FEELINGS	————	

continued

VI. Knowledge/Experience

I have skills or knowledge, either through formal or informal education, to perform this task	YES	NO
I have or will receive recognition, awards, or praise for performing well on this task	YES	NO
I have work experience related to this task	YES	NO
I volunteer or am willing to volunteer to do this task	YES	NO
I may be tired at the end of the day, but performing this task does not drain me		

TOTAL TOTALKNOWLEDGE/EXPERIENCE   _____

TOTAL OVERALL YESes _____   TOTAL OVERALL NOs _____

Part 2: Your Observations Based on Your Results

In what areas did you have more YESes than NOs? In what areas are you heavily weighted as a YES or NO and why do you think that is?

_____

_____

_____

_____

_____

_____

_____

_____

How do you feel overall about the results? Is it how you perceive yourself on a daily basis versus how you really feel internally? Any surprises?

_____

_____

_____

_____

_____

_____

_____

Are you using your inner talents, strengths, abilities, gifts, and experiences to your full potential in the work you are doing?

_____

_____

_____

_____

_____

Part 3: Set an Intention on Where to Refocus to Align Your Inner Self to Your Work

_____

_____

BREAKING BELIEFS PODCAST SPOTLIGHT
Pillow Talk: Creating Awareness of the Self-Doubt to Get to the Truth

Joseph Oniwor, a former pro arena football player turned break-through transformational trainer, has been in the fitness industry for several years. He focuses on helping people regain confidence within themselves. Oniwor is a firm believer that if you incorporate mindfulness, holistic lifestyle changes, and a healthy workout regimen into your life, your passion will become a reality.

In terms of formulating your backstory, Oniwor suggests beginning with what he calls "pillow talk."

How do you talk to yourself before bed—that pillow talk of truth? As he explains, "Would you be best friends with yourself if you pay attention to the things you say to yourself?" Pillow talk can help you answer that question.

He uses this concept with himself and his training clients. He'll say to them, "Let me work out with you for 30 minutes. Don't tell me anything about you, and [yet] you'll tell me all about your life. I'll know everything about you in 30 minutes of a hard workout."

To answer your pillow talk question, you must first become aware of the inner conversation that creates your negative auto response. He explains: "For me, it's like that glass ceiling or that fake ceiling where I always stumble. In the book *The Big Leap* [by Gay Hendricks], this is called the Upper Limit—you hit your upper limit, and you start doing the same thing. That will bring you back down to that comfort zone or that paradigm belief. However, once you're aware of it, you can make a choice to say, 'Is this true? Is this not true? Can I move forward?'

"For instance, I get to make a decision, and you said, 'I don't think you could do that.' I don't know if I'm good enough. But is this really true?

"But I have a body of sports performance that says, 'I am good enough. This is not true.'

"Where did this new awareness come from? When I wasn't picked first on the playground, I decided I wasn't good enough to play with everybody else. It seems trivial, but many people have had the greatest ability. Still, they face a situation like this, and it stops at being just a manager when they could have been a CEO. That awareness of pillow talk is the number one thing that allows that."

He continues: "When I'm training my athletes, that's the number one thing we focus on. If something comes up, if we're doing a heavy set or finishing up, and I notice a cue, I'll immediately say, 'What's that? What came up right there? What were you thinking?'

"It will be an opportunity for them to say, 'This is what it was.' We may go into that in the space or bring awareness. A couple of weeks later, they come back and say, 'You asked me what I got scared about there. I noticed that I saw that in three different areas.'

"The brain only knows effort or situation. It doesn't say, 'You're in a gym. You're good here. You're at home with the husband; you're not good there.' It only knows one thing. Once you become aware of it, you see how it's starting to play out, and you can powerfully choose."

To hear the full interview with Joseph Oniwor, visit:

https://www.amyvetter.com/breakingbeliefspodcast/
episode-57-pillow-talk-creating-awareness-of-the-self-doubt-
to-get-to-the-truth-with-joseph-oniwor.

⚔ MINDFUL MOMENTS

- Everyone has a backstory, and it's up to each of us to change that narrative when it doesn't serve us. When you read this chapter, did any backstories come up for you? If so, document it.

- I began this work because I realized that something felt off internally that I couldn't identify. I found that my own backstory of feeling unheard led to work that I needed to do in the future to value my needs.

- No matter what stories our parents and grandparents chose to live with, we have the option to break those patterns and live out our dreams by doing work on ourselves. We can learn to break through those patterns without using those backstories as a reason why we do or don't do something or treat someone in a way that we didn't intend.

- It's up to us to break through fear, belief systems, and other inherited tendencies that might be holding us back. Doing this work is the biggest gift we can give to ourselves and those around us. We not only create a better experience for ourselves but are better for the people around us, and we can empathize with the experiences they have that may be holding them back.

CHAPTER 2

Our Internal Stories Create Our Habits—and Vice Versa

"If you cannot admit you have a problem, you're not ready to make the change. If you still don't believe you have a problem, then the negative consequences of your behavior haven't become real enough for you."

—BENJAMIN HARDY

Whether we admit it or not, many of our internal stories and patterns we bring into the workplace come from our childhood. When we go through change, we often don't step back and observe why we believe what we do or what holds us back.

Are these beliefs our own or what we were told to believe growing up? As I have learned over time through the stories and my research presented in this book, we often do not know what each person carries with them and how that affects them—at any moment—personally or at work.

The human condition often includes the stories of our own suffering. These stories stick to us and replay in a constant loop in our mind. We may not realize how these stories affect us at work or home until we step back, review our situation, and understand what triggers our responses.

We can find ourselves living in a repeating loop, as portrayed in the movie *Groundhog Day*. Do you find yourself receiving similar feedback—

- With each job?
- With each boss?
- With friends?
- With those you love?

What consistent feedback do you experience over and over at work? Do you blame the outside world without taking a hard look at how your backstory affects you? Do you resist change because of the habits you created in life, and the effort to change them seems impossible?

When we are unhappy with an outcome, it is human nature to blame the outside world for our circumstances. It is rare to step back and review ourselves and resolve the reason for patterns that show up in our lives, whether at work, at home, or internally. Or alternatively, we may choose to be too hard on ourselves and internalize rather than get a realistic view of the situation.

Suppose we don't do the work and don't review our personal circumstances. In that case, we risk bringing habits into the workplace or (like in my personal experience) into the next generation of those we care about. As with anything new or when we experience pain, we create a lot of internal fear of the unknown and create stories of what might happen—and then we worry. We often feel despair when we think about the future and don't know where to turn. However, we *can* initiate change, though embracing it can sometimes be painful as we try to get to the other side of it.

CHANGING HABITS

Changing our perspective from "How will this affect me?" to "How will this affect those around me?" can be a small shift that not only benefits ourselves, but those around us.

The human mind doesn't like uncertainty or discomfort. Our typical response to distress is to run away, avoid, eliminate, control, lash out, or resist. This creates behaviors like procrastination, over- or under-eating, distraction, busyness, clutter, financial problems, avoiding exercise and self-care, and more.

We tend to take our own limited view of life, based on past experiences, and don't think about it from other perspectives or consider approaching something in a new way. To get there, it's up to us to take an honest look at ourselves and identify the repeated patterns or habits that may prevent our progress.

But first, let's begin with what a "habit" is.

The definition of a habit from the *Merriam-Webster* dictionary is the following:

- A settled tendency or usual manner of behavior

- An acquired mode of behavior that has become nearly or completely involuntary

- An addiction
- A behavior pattern acquired by frequent repetition
  or physiologic exposure that shows itself in regularity
  or increased facility of performance

We often want to change how we show up in life or find a way to break a behavior; yet more often than not, rather than change, we simply go on repeating the same habit.

However, when we take time to step back, pause, and review our situation, we can better understand what triggers us to respond in the specific ways we would like to avoid.

Because of my own family dynamics, I grew up protecting the behaviors of my family members. I tried to help them while at the same time pretending to the outside world that everything was fine. I have learned that when we experience trauma, we protect the people who harm us and often don't speak up. This is because we feel bad or don't want them to feel bad. The result is that we harbor their secrets, which in turn creates turmoil in our own lives.

Growing up, I looked up to my mom. As far as I can remember, I put her first, even before my friends, because I loved her so much. I saw her as this strong and independent woman that I imagined myself to be one day. She owned a successful maid service with locations in three cities. I began working in her business when I was 12. I was dropped off from the bus and went straight to work. I loved being in the office with her and learned so much from her about business. There were many lessons I learned from her that I still use today, such as putting yourself out there at net-working events to make the contacts you need in business.

It can still be uncomfortable for me to walk into a room

where I don't know anyone and begin meeting people. Whenever I feel that way, I often remember watching my mom work a room and meet people, which gives me the confidence to push through the experience myself. I also remember watching her as a business owner go through the ups and downs of running a company and not giving in when things were tough or not perfect. I have had to summon that up internally many times in business when going through hard times to not let it beat me and to remain optimistic. Watching and learning from her gave me the confidence to create the career I have today.

When I was young, there weren't a lot of women entrepreneurs or business leaders that I could look up to. My mom's career made me think that one day I could become a business owner myself. I thought it was amazing that a woman could run a business, and I dreamed of being just like her and having a career. Experiencing her business made it possible in my head that I could do the same. However, despite all the positive lessons I learned from her, I had to overcome many issues in our personal relationship to become the person I am now.

My mother would say to me from the time I was a young child, "I know you are going to leave me one day, just like everyone else does in my life." I was fiercely loyal to her and constantly felt the need to prove it to her. There never seemed to be enough I could do, though, to prove my love.

I felt lucky to be my mom's confidant. She shared with me stories that would later serve as excuses she would use for why she mistreated me.

One particular story let her off the hook every time. When she was eight, my mother was kidnapped while walking to the movie theater with her friend. At the time, it was normal for kids her age to walk around without supervision. From what she told me, she was recovered safely a few days later and the kidnapper eventually went to jail.

She told me this story over and over throughout my life. She told me every detail except for what happened while she was kidnapped; she left that to my imagination. Until the day my grandfather died, he ensured that the man who kidnapped her remained in jail anytime he was up for a release of his sentence.

Her experience ended up being a story that not only affected her, but also eventually affected me and everyone who ever became close to her. From what I was told by her, I believe her parents had her go to therapy as a child. However, to my knowledge, she never went back to therapy as an adult. Every time I brought up that she should consider talking to someone, she refused. She said therapy was for "weak" people.

So instead, she leaned on me. I was the one with whom she shared her most personal and horrifying stories. This made me feel responsible for her well-being—to protect her against any harm. It forced me to make excuses for her when she treated me or anyone else around me badly.

I went through hoops throughout my life trying to prove my loyalty to her, no matter how she treated me. She would continually bring up her past experiences of people "leaving her" or mistreating her. She believed that you never forgive, and you walk away from people when they treat you poorly and never look back. I was always afraid she would turn her back on me one day, so I did everything to show my devotion.

- I became a CPA because her father was a CPA, and it would make her happy.

- I played violin because her father played violin, and that would make her happy.

- I excelled at school so she would be happy.

- After my parents divorced, I took care of my brothers and gave up my own social activities in high school so she could have the freedom she needed to go out on dates and socialize with her friends.

- I showed her she was number one in my life, whether with my friendships, boyfriends, my prior marriage, or children. Yes, even my children.

I moved out when I married at 23. Once I was no longer living with her, I spoke with her at least three or four times a day. I considered her my best friend, even though, when I look back, it seemed she was mad at me most of the time and I couldn't make her happy, and many of those calls ended with her hanging up on me.

SHIFTING ROLES PRESENT A NEW CHALLENGE

Being pregnant with my first child presented the next hurdle to clear with my mom. She viewed every relationship in my life as a threat to the one we had. In her mind, now there would be another person—my baby—who could potentially replace her in my heart. I remember how excited I was to tell her I was having a baby. I had a special cookie cake made so when she opened it, she would read the message that she was going to be a grandparent. Instead of being elated, she was upset and angry. She later admitted that I wasn't mistaken. She was trying to understand her place as a grandmother and how a new baby would take attention away from her, rather than having the desire to be part of the experience.

My pregnancy did not go well. I ended up in preterm labor three months early and on bed rest, and then my son arrived six weeks early. He had wires and tubes everywhere. He was in the NICU initially and then later back in the PICU because of being a preemie and the health issues resulting from it. As I learned growing up, to get through any hard times I kept my head down and focused on pushing through and tried not to think of the worst.

When he was finally home, he was not in great shape. He had dislocated hips, so his knees were strapped to his sides like a frog to get his hip joints to form correctly. He had an apnea monitor where an alarm would sound in case he stopped breathing. He was jaundiced and colicky.

One day, I walked him in a stroller with the cover up to shade him. A woman stopped me and said, "Let me see the baby!" When I opened the stroller, she gasped because of all the wires strapped to and around him. I remember reassuring *her* that he was fine. Everything was fine.

However, I was scared. Right then, when I needed my mom the most, she was not there to help, despite the many times I asked.

I tried to figure out my work situation and felt panicked.

How would I be a good mom with a preemie and still have the career I had envisioned for myself? My mother took this opportunity to feed into my insecurities as a new mom, saying my baby connected more with his dad than with me and she could tell that my baby didn't love me. I was so out of sorts, tired, stressed, and scared, that I believed her. Later I realized that she did this so I would feel more connected to her than to my new family.

After having my second child, at age 32, I broke down. He was my second preemie, and I got quite sick after this pregnancy and was hospitalized. My mom didn't come to help when I needed her. Instead of helping and taking care of me, she told me I was faking being sick. My then-husband and I were scrambling to take care of both children and my health, as well as ensure our careers stayed on track since we had no fallback and there was no one else to help.

I was disappointed and lost. I thought I would share my children with my mom in this next phase of my life, but instead, she saw them as yet another test of my loyalty to her, and I would need to put her ahead of them. I realized I couldn't make her happy. I would never be able to do enough to prove to her that I loved her.

I felt off but couldn't identify what was wrong. I decided I needed to see a therapist. To do that, though, I had to break past the belief my mother had instilled in me that therapy was for weak people. I eventually found that seeing a mental health professional is one of the most courageous acts you can do for yourself and the people around you. I didn't want to end up repeating the destructive patterns of my parents and their parents before them. I realized I needed help to ensure I wouldn't.

During one of my initial visits, my therapist said, "You need to divorce your mother."

I didn't want to do that because of all the generations before me that didn't speak to their family members. I wanted my children to have a different experience than I did and have all their family in their life. So instead, I made minor adjustments. First, I reduced the number of times I spoke to her in a day. With just that little change, she went on the offensive. My brother ended up repeating stories to me about how she was making fun of me to him and talked disparagingly about me. She also began to speak badly about me to my children even while I was present, who were in preschool and elementary school, old enough to tell me about it. Once this reality came to fruition, I had no choice but to not allow my children to be subjected to this generational pattern of behavior and to think it is okay to treat people you supposedly love like this.

Once I shared my stories of my mother, father, and their parents with my therapist, he educated me on a concept called "epigenetics"—how people's behaviors and their environment can change their genes. In epigenetics, the idea is that past trauma can leave a chemical mark on a person's genes, which then can be passed from generation to generation. The genes are not damaged, just altered. This can result in the children of trauma survivors also experiencing their own trauma from these "survivors" or the previous generation (grandparents), which leaves them exposed to various possible health issues—physical, mental, and emotional.

As Eva Fogelman, a "second generation" child as well as a psychologist, has said, "there's a Second Generation Complex that affects our identity, self-esteem, interpersonal interactions, and worldview. Our past either drives us or traps us, sometimes in subtle ways, often subconsciously. That's why knowing the patterns and behaviors of your family-of-origin is so important to understand how you became who you are and how that impacts your relationships."[3]

When we acknowledge these stories in our lives, we can see how they affect our work and home life. The effects of epigenetics can be the same, based on the different traumas your parents may have experienced and how they transferred that to you. But first, we need to recognize that it is happening for us.

When we recognize these triggers that create our own habits and behaviors in the world, it's up to us to find a way to acknowledge them. The next step is then to understand how we can reprogram our natural tendencies to approach life differently.

FAMILY KARMA

As author and spiritual teacher Sara Wiseman says in her article "Release Yourself from Family Karma," "If you don't release yourself from family karma, you can't become free . . . releasing ourselves from family karma is a process that takes us from anger and pain to compassion and healing."[4]

When we create more compassion for ourselves, it creates space to have more compassion for those around us. It opens

---

3 https://evafogelman.com/publications/group-belonging-and-mourning/.

4 https://mailchi.mp/124ff855b24e/8va8tc6qa8-951884

our eyes to connect differently with the people in our personal lives and who we work with. We have a deeper understanding that everyone has these stories that create our behaviors and can affect how we work, interact, and lead. When we muster up compassion for ourselves, we can begin to transform our own backstory—for ourselves and the world.

To begin this journey to better understand each other, we first have to uncover who we really are without the outside noise and expectations. As adults, we often don't determine what *we* believe, rather than what we were told to think growing up. When we recognize these old beliefs, we can begin to question how these show up at work or in our personal lives. Then we can decide whether we agree with that belief system or choose to create a clean slate and go about things differently. Do our interactions produce a positive result? Or do we need an approach to achieve better outcomes?

Breaking habits sometimes comes down to understanding the internal stories that drive us and the decisions we make. So often, it's hard for us to make a change because we're safe where we are and it is what we know.

I began to recognize how my internal stories affected my career decisions and how I viewed my family and friends, even being a mother. All through growing up my passion was in art and music.

My mom decided to become an art teacher when she went to college but told me many times that it had been a mistake and she should have become an accountant like my grandfather. I heard many stories of my grandfather's career as a CPA from my mother as I grew up and how it was considered a safe and stable profession. Coming from an immigrant family, my grand-father helped his family and the next generation to be better off because of the career he chose.

When it was time to select a major in college, rather than go to art school, I enrolled in business school to become an accountant. Even though I wanted to go into a creative field, that was not an option that my mom would allow. I do have to say that the decision to be an accountant definitely created an excellent career for me and my family. Because of watching my parents lose everything, I always had an internal fear of the same happening to me one day. Therefore, I agreed to play it safe and not follow the career I desired.

I would see other art students on campus and feel a pang of envy in my heart. But I quickly shut it down. I knew the future I wanted. I stayed focused and worked hard on a degree that didn't come naturally to me.

In college, I asked everyone whether I should specialize in audit or tax. I didn't know what either one really was. I followed the guidance of others and continued to play it safe.

I began a traditional accounting career as an auditor and it was going well. When my first son was born early and was a preemie, I initially thought nothing was going to change. I would keep doing what I was doing and continue to move up the ranks in my career.

But then, after the ordeal with my son, I realized I couldn't go back to my old job and work schedule because of the care he required at that time. The funny thing is, at the time, I actually asked the company for a flexible schedule when I returned from maternity leave. Their response was that I could work from 8 a.m. to 5 p.m. in the office—and then work from home from 6 p.m. to 10 p.m. Needless to say, that was not going to work!

So, I decided to go back to my roots as an entrepreneur and take a small step toward not playing it safe and instead take my first risk and launch my own accounting business.

Even though I had an audit background, when I researched starting up a business I quickly realized there was more liability with an audit practice. I decided I didn't want to take on that liability alone, which led to my decision to hire bookkeepers and offer bookkeeping services instead. I looked up how other accountants and CPAs advertised themselves and saw that they were certified in an accounting software. So, I did the same.

One of my first potential clients called and said they didn't want my business to do their bookkeeping but instead wanted help on how to better understand their financials produced by the accounting software they used. When I visited them, they asked me questions about how to use the software differently and how it impacted the results they saw on the financials. Since I was new in business, I actually hadn't learned the software enough to answer with any confidence. So instead I said, "You know what, I'll get back to you on that."

I went home and researched their questions. The next day, I called the client and answered with what they needed. And guess what? They were happy and felt I delivered what they needed. This experience changed how I offered future services. First, I learned as an entrepreneur that we create a business, and then our customers inform us about what they need versus what we think they need. To keep them happy, it's important to pivot to meet clients' needs. Secondly, I found I could be transparent and let people know when I am not entirely sure of an answer as long as they feel confident I know how to find what they need and be responsive and timely with a solution.

By breaking through my internal stories about playing it safe, and being okay with not needing to be an immediate expert or perfect, I realized that people wanted my advice, not the numbers I gave them. They wanted me to help them understand their businesses better and help them make decisions with my expertise.

We all have that unique skill to offer others. We just need to be open to listening to what they ask and whether we can deliver. I found learning what they wanted me to know provided an opportunity to create new, exciting types of services that combined my creative and business sides. I also learned that it was okay to make mistakes, and it was unrealistic to be perfect all the time. (See *Breaking Beliefs* Podcast Spotlight: "Do Your Best and, Yes, It's Okay to Make Mistakes," highlighted at the end of this chapter.)

If I hadn't taken this leap of faith to begin a business where I wasn't an expert or taken on clients who had requests that created new service lines I never imagined, I would not have the rewarding career I now enjoy. Being open to learning and growing is something I do over and over. It's not always perfect, but I have learned that I thrive in the climb and solving puzzles to achieve my goals. I also have found the self-confidence that I will figure it out even when things go sideways and backward at times.

I chose my career based on what I saw as a child of a business owner and a granddaughter of a CPA. When I speak at conferences, I ask the audiences that are accounting and financial professionals why they chose their profession. The top three responses are:

1. My family member was an accountant or financial professional.
2. I was good at math.
3. It was a safe career.

Then there are always those people who like to joke around and respond—*to impress the girls!*

Many times this is more about what we are familiar with from our history or what skills we possess rather than the value we want to create. We are all more than what we do in our careers. Learning what excites my teammates, and why they do what they do, has been an important step in connecting with those around me. I have found it is essential to know the people I work with on a more personal level, and that begins with uncovering their outside interests and hobbies. This way, we can be more united as a team and allow everyone's unique talents to shine through. This breaks down barriers so our team can succeed.

There was a time when I felt like I couldn't expose my outside interests and hobbies at work. I didn't tell anyone that I practiced and taught yoga, especially since I was a CPA, a traditionally conservative profession. On the other hand, I didn't let my yoga students know I was a CPA by day. However, one day that changed.

An accounting client of mine walked into my yoga class. She was so surprised to see me as the teacher, she began to talk with me about work and the other students overheard. Then the questions began:

"Are you a . . . CPA?"

"I had no idea . . . my husband is a CPA."

"My friend is an accountant."

"I need an accountant!"

It then occurred to me to bring all of my sides together. My co-workers and clients found me more interesting at work once we could connect about our outside interests and what we had in common. There was no reason to separate it. If anything, this sharing created deeper bonds and brought more purpose into the working relationship.

THE "RIGHT-BRAINED" WAY OF THINKING

These interests and hobbies are even more important than you might think in our high-tech world. In his book *A Whole New Mind: Why Right-Brainers Will Rule the Future*, Daniel H. Pink discusses the importance of building our creative (or right-brained) skills because human innovation is more valuable than ever.[5] While more logic-centric thinking will still have its place, Pink argues that the left-brained skills will be overshadowed by outsourcing and automation. The more artistic and big-picture right-brained individuals will need to teach and share these skills with their left-brain-learning counterparts. And those left-brainers will have to flex their creativity to maintain a competitive edge in business.

5 New York: Penguin/Riverhead, 2006.

Creativity often is an underutilized and misunderstood business skill. Creativity doesn't always mean traditional forms of expression like dance, art, and music. It can also mean innovative thinking, deep analysis, and problem-solving.

Tapping into our personal interests and hobbies helps us to strengthen our creative side and remember how to learn so we can positively influence workplace innovation. You can practice "design" without becoming a graphic designer. Flexing this particular creative muscle means thinking about how the world is designed. For example, think about your local grocery store's layout, how the controls are placed in a car, and the order in which items appear on a menu. Once you notice how your surroundings are designed, and question the way things are, you are more curious about the world around you and you think about ways of improving it.

After all, art is not necessarily painting and music. It's creating something that wasn't there before.

RETURNING TO THE B³ METHOD

These outside hobbies also help us return to the beginner's mind to innovate and create. It is the cornerstone of the B³ Method®, described in my book *Business, Balance & Bliss: How the B³ Method® Can Transform Your Career and Life.* The B³ Method® is an equation: *Business + Balance = Bliss.* It works like this:

The *Business* part is the stressful situations we encounter each workday, such as deadlines, challenging personalities, technology transformation, striving for that promotion, and more.

The *Balance* is the natural tool we have internally to reset

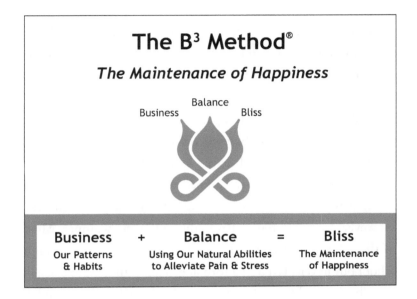

The B³ Method®

The Maintenance of Happiness

Business   Balance   Bliss

Business	**+**	**Balance**	**=**	**Bliss**
Our Patterns & Habits		Using Our Natural Abilities to Alleviate Pain & Stress		The Maintenance of Happiness

ourselves to intentionally create the energy we want to put out in the world. By using our natural abilities we can show up with the people around us in a positive way.

This leads to creating our *Bliss*, or how we maintain happiness. Rather than expecting happiness to occur accidentally, we work to regulate ourselves and ensure we create joy and contentment in our business and personal lives. Hence, we make a better experience for everyone in our intimate circle.

Business + Balance = Bliss also helps us connect to our creative side at work, to innovate when we need to.

As children, we were constantly learning something new, and our minds had to be agile. Even if we weren't good at something, we had to keep doing it. That is what changes when we become adults. We become experts in our vocations, and we resist being a beginner and learning again. But to create an environment of innovation, we have to allow ourselves to learn again and be uncomfortable. As Connected Leaders, we need to create an environment where learning can happen without consequence.

I did this as an adult and pushed myself out of my comfort zone with an outside hobby when I decided to learn the bass guitar. Even though I had played violin and viola growing up, my real love was rock! So, I signed up for lessons and joined an adult performance band. They told me it was for beginners. However, I quickly found I was the only true beginner. Most of the other men there had played guitar privately since high school but never played in a formal group, so they were considered "beginners." It was frustrating to be the only one who didn't know what they were doing.

However, I needed to be uncomfortable, so I could learn. I reminded myself at the end of each day that I wanted to play the bass guitar. And when we actually played our first concert, it was exhilarating! It wasn't about being the best or perfect; it was about the experience and learning along the way.

As leaders, we have to remember what it is like to discover new things for the first time. We do not always have to provide the answer to questions people ask; instead, we can empower them to be self-sufficient and understand how they learn, so we can guide them and expand their knowledge. It is harder to be open-minded and present once we have gained expertise, rather than cutting people off because their ideas haven't worked in the past, or choosing to give orders instead.

To be true Connected Leaders—leaders who listen to, support, and nurture others—we help others realize their potential and push them to grow and thrive and break through what holds them back. Sometimes it takes time for them to figure it out themselves. Still, it's vital for them to "Go Fish" so you can see how they find and analyze situations and create new services or products, rather than giving them the answer prematurely because you already know how to solve the issue. By allowing a team to come up with their own answer, I have discovered that they can sometimes arrive at an even better idea or find a better path. When we are uncomfortable is often the time when we learn and grow the most.

It is crucial to create an environment that allows people to test and fail without being branded as failures for the rest of their careers. The only way for innovation to happen is to create a safe space for people to break their habit, get creative, and try new ideas without harming their livelihood or personal brand.

When we change our perspective and patterns, we are open to new opportunities and finally stop playing it safe. Taking risks in an educated way can help you break through the patterns that you brought into adulthood. Trying something new to see what happens is something to embrace rather than fear.

RELEASING THE WOUNDS

The second part of family karma work is about releasing the wounds that we carry. Many people have experienced abuse or trauma in their families or as a child. This process is about learning not to be a victim. If we were abused or have encountered any type of trauma, releasing ourselves from family karma means stepping into our own power.

The importance of this is—

1. We don't want to look to be a victim or focus on negative interactions.

2. We don't want to accept being a victim if mistreated by a boss or co-worker.

3. We don't want to operate in fear; for instance, assuming any change will eliminate our importance at work or in our lives.

In the workplace, knowing that most have experienced some form of trauma can change how we may respond to one another. How can we find ways to develop more compassion for others and see each other as humans, not just as our co-workers? How could this change the way we interact, solve problems, innovate, and create?

In a favorite book of mine, *The Wisdom of Yoga* by Stephen Cope, liberation is defined as "freedom from all the sources of conditioning that bind us to small ways of thinking and being."[6]

Cope writes that "Liberation means to be entirely awake and fully alive . . . Yogis believed that the ordinary reality in which most human beings live is merely an elaborate construction based on subtle but important errors in perception. It is possible to become gradually disentangled from these habits, and as we do, to see more clearly, and to experience less suffering. The process is not easy. It requires a considerable amount

6   *The Wisdom of Yoga: A Seeker's Guide to Extraordinary Living* (New York: Bantam, 2006).

of effort, cultivation of insight and subtle mental and physical skillfulness."

The fantastic thing about all of this is that it's not new. The human condition to release ourselves from suffering, interact more peacefully, detach from trying to control a situation, and be more aware of how we affect others has been around for thousands of years. With a deeper awareness of ourselves and how we affect others, we can create a positive family and work environment, lead more mindfully, and be more present for those around us.

B³ BREAK

1. What is one habit or pattern that you notice showing up in your life? How has this affected your mindset or how you interact with people? Identifying it can help you focus on where you need to make a change.

2. How have beliefs from your family been passed to your generation and affected you and those around you? Knowing where your "bad" habits or behavior may originate can provide the insight you need to begin altering your approach to personal and professional relationships.

3. "Monkey mind" can create negative stories in our heads that are not true. When that harmful thinking arises, disconnect by walking, meditating, or listening to music.

BREAKING BELIEFS PODCAST SPOTLIGHT
Do Your Best and, Yes, It's Okay to Make Mistakes

A great work ethic helps with success, but what you learn along the way can help you grow as a leader and a person. Grace Horvath, president and CEO at CPAmerica, a national not-for-profit trade association that serves independent CPA firms, has learned many valuable lessons during her long career in business development, marketing, and sales. Here are a few that have stood out.

Include people in the process. While working in sales at Christian Dior early in her career, Horvath discovered that how you approach sales is similar to cultivating other business and team relationships. For instance, in sales, she says that "you figure out what are [the customer's] pain points and how to help enhance them so that they feel like you're not being sold to, or you're not being led in a certain way, so they feel they're part of the process."

Walk the talk. Horvath has also learned that defining and showing your personal level of excellence helps inspire your employees and co-workers. "It shows what people can expect of her and what she expects of others," she says. This commitment carries over to all aspects of her life. "Whether I invited you over and I'm making you a meal or working on a PowerPoint presentation or putting together a project that you're doing, you don't want to turn out something mediocre," she says. "Especially to the point that it's obvious, like, 'This person didn't even try.'"

Do your best even if you fall short. "That's always something that I told my children growing up," she says. "It's not about getting the A; it's that you did your best. Even if you got an A-minus, that was more right if you think you did your best. You have to be proud of yourself."

It's okay to make mistakes. For anyone who wants to climb high and someday become a partner or managing partner, people have to be able to trust you on every level, she says. "They have to know that you're going to do what you say you're going to do. They have to know that you are reliable and accountable. It's okay to let people see you be vulnerable. Even if you're at or near the top, let people know when you've made a mistake and when something is your fault. Then say, 'this is how we're going to get through this and go to the next level.'"

To hear the full interview with Grace Horvath, visit:

https://www.amyvetter.com/breakingbeliefspodcast/
episode-8-do-your-best-its-okay-when-you-make-mistakes-
along-the-way-with-grace-horvath.

♨ MINDFUL MOMENTS

- It's human nature to blame our current situation on our circumstances, but it's far more helpful to take a look at how we got there. We tend to take our own limited view of life, based on past experiences and beliefs we've grown up with.

- To change this, we need to take an honest look at ourselves and identify the repeated patterns or habits—and belief systems that have been handed down through the generations—that may be preventing our progress. We can identify whether our beliefs are our own or someone else's that are affecting our actions.

- Finding an outside third party, such as a trained therapist, can help you decipher patterns and beliefs that are not serving you and instead create the outcomes you desire.

- At work, the Connected Leader listens, supports, and nurtures their team. This means being open to letting the team come up with their own way of doing things, rather than expecting them to follow the status quo.

- Family karma can be debilitating if we carry old wounds and let fear stop us from moving forward. By releasing old wounds we can instead carry compassion for ourselves and others.

CHAPTER 3

Perception versus Reality

"Struggle changes an ordinary human into a spiritually awake person."
—SWAMI KRIPALU

As we move through the ranks of business, we get less and less feedback. This causes us to sometimes misunderstand how others view us and whether they see us as being aligned with how we feel internally.

I have found that just because we don't ask those around us for feedback on how they perceive us or how we treat them doesn't mean they don't talk about it to each other. It's much better to create an environment where you can have an open conversation to gain a better understanding and clarity around other people's viewpoints and be open to what they have to say.

We can also learn a lot about ourselves from looking internally and realizing how our self-perception may not be aligned with how others view us. This comes down to our perception

versus reality. Rather than getting defensive about other perspectives, we can instead focus on receiving feedback to help us
gain a better understanding of ourselves and then decide how
we utilize that information.

When I was in fourth grade, my mom had a musician friend
on *The Tonight Show*. He heard of an opportunity on a Disney
Channel show he thought would be a good fit for me. The theme
of the show was that children would write in with a wish, and
the show would try to fulfill it.

One child wrote that they wanted to build a sandcastle of
the Magic Kingdom. My mom's friend knew the show's director, and instead of granting the "real" child's wish, they "found"
a child who had certain qualities they were looking for. In this
particular instance, they found me instead. This was when I first
learned that what we think is reality may not always be true.

I was so excited—I was going to Hollywood! When my
mom and I arrived, we went to an office where I got an actor's
permit. While I sat in the waiting room, I admired all the famous
children's pictures hanging on the wall. I was in awe.

The show hired a world champion sand sculptor to help me
build a 14-foot-tall sandcastle. The night before the TV shoot,
my mom and I went to Chinatown with her friend. At dinner,
her friend disclosed that no one knew that I was not the "real"
child that made the wish. I needed to lie to everyone that I wrote
the letter. The staff didn't know, nor did the sand sculptor. Only
his friend who was the director knew. He put a ton of pressure on me that I would make him look bad if I told the truth.
My fourth-grade self felt internally frustrated and finally spoke
up and said, "I am going to make myself look bad too if I tell

the truth." My mom explained that this was how Hollywood worked, and most of what I saw on TV is not real.

I was not only disappointed but also scared I was going to screw up. The sand sculptor was excited to be there, which made me feel horrible the whole day for lying to him. After more than 14 hours, TV reporters interviewed us when we finished building the sandcastle. One asked him why he would do something like this, and his response was that he was so amazed that a child would have this wish, and he was excited to be a part of it. I felt so bad that night.

When I got home, there was publicity in the local newspapers, and I was invited to a local TV talk show in my hometown. The day of my interview, I waited in the show's green room with my parents before being interviewed live by the host. My parents reminded me to stick to what the show told me to say. I also knew my fourth-grade class was scheduled to watch me on TV when it was going to air. I was so nervous I was going to say the wrong thing, so, needless to say, this was one of the worst interviews ever. Whenever the host asked a question, I would nod or answer "yes" or "no" with minimal description. For someone who was always in trouble with teachers for talking too much in class, it was the first time I had nothing to say. I made it really hard on the host interviewing me who was just doing his job.

Everyone only knew what they saw. They did not know the backstory of the situation. They only witnessed a less than stellar interview and had no way of knowing the truth of my experience. They were led to believe what they were supposed to.

I share this story because it's similar to what we see today with social media profiles. How do we appear to our friends and family? How do we put ourselves forward to our work colleagues and other people in our professions? We don't necessarily share what we don't want people to know. And sometimes, we begin to believe what we want others to think rather than identifying who we *really* are.

But we also do the opposite. We perceive others the way they want to be seen, making us form opinions (good and bad) without knowing reality.

So ask yourself: What is your truth? How can you connect with it? How do you maintain your integrity through each of your decisions? How can you see others deeper than what is shown at face value?

FINDING THE TRUTH

Every day, we tell stories about what happens to us at work and home. Our perception is often different from others who tell the same story. So, where is the truth?

Typically, a story has many layers, and often we don't take the time to learn other people's sides of the same story. It is natural to justify our own side of a story rather than look at all sides. To reach the truth often means letting go of the ego and taking responsibility for our part of the story and how we influence it. We may not want to admit it, but finding the truth often comes down to how we manage our ego.

In Stephen Cope's book *The Wisdom of Yoga*, he describes two facets of the ego. One is the ideal external state that we long for. This is made up of images and feelings we've collected throughout life and connects to an internal state of happiness we have fleetingly experienced. The longing for this happiness can be powerful. But it's an unconscious desire, and we often don't understand how it drives us.

The second facet of the ego is composed of unconscious ideas of who we are. This type of ego makes us deny certain essential realities. It defends itself and keeps our view of brutal truths or reality obscured.

These internalized viewpoints of our "self" can be the root causes of unhappiness and delusion—in our work and personal life. However, with focused practice, the unrealistic representations of the ideal ego can be exposed and deconstructed.

I mentioned earlier that my brothers and I took the brunt of our father's temper. I actually had a closer relationship with my father than my brothers did growing up, and I've always thought it was because I was the first child and the only girl. He coached all of our sports teams. So, from the outside, everyone thought we had a great relationship.

But they didn't know what happened when no one was looking. My father was disappointed because I was never a good enough athlete at any sport he coached. He embarrassed me in front of my teammates by making fun of me when I messed up and often commented how he was in awe of other girls that were the team's star players. I wished I could be just like the girls he admired, but I knew I was never going to measure up.

His temper grew worse over the years as his relationship with my mom deteriorated. He confided in me about how he felt about my mom. But I observed he wouldn't necessarily get angry at her. Instead, he took his anger out on me, mostly because I was the one around when she was traveling for work, but also, I think, because I reminded him of her.

I knew my father deeply loved my mom; however, as their relationship worsened, so did his treatment of me. After each episode of my father lashing out, we went days without speaking and walked past each other in silence many times in the house. I stayed in my room as much as possible. Typically, about three days after he acted out, he would apologize. He often broke down and cried and blamed his behavior on his parents' treatment of him, which often made me feel sorry for him.

I did not know his parents (my grandparents from Arizona) but heard stories from him and my mother. Apparently, my grandmother mistreated everyone—my father, family members, and even strangers.

But if you looked deeper and peeled back the layers, there was a reason for her bad behavior as well. The story that was passed down was that when she was 12, my grandmother from Arizona and her two younger brothers were placed in an orphanage. As she told it to my dad, their mother (my great-grandmother) simply dropped them off and then drove away to California.

Doing some research on my family history on Ancestry.com, I found there was more detailed information about my great-grandmother and her life, which included finding my grandmother's and her siblings' birth certificates. One birth certificate showed my great-grandmother was 16 years old when she had my grandmother. Her husband was much older. By age 21, she had given birth to four children, but one had died.

By the time she placed her children in the orphanage and left for California for a "new" life, it was the Great Depression.

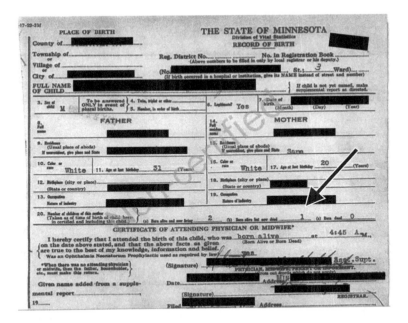

Ancestry.com also showed that her husband was living in what would be considered a poorhouse and had to share a room at that time.

I developed a different perspective of my great-grandmother with all these new facts. She may have had no other way to care for her children—we will never know for sure. However, the impact of her decision to abandon them at the orphanage was the story passed down through the generations. The trauma affected my grandmother, and in turn, her behavior affected my father, and then his behavior affected my brothers and me. Each generation lived in the wake of that story and manipulated the truth to excuse their own actions. That is where the ego becomes too powerful, and we lose our sense of reality and personal responsibility.

When you review your own life, what stories have been passed down that have created patterns of behavior in your family that may or may not be true? If that story was proven to have different sides, how would that change you or the people around you?

THE "I" IN EGO

Our ego can easily spill over into our work lives and how we interact with others. We become attached to a belief system about ourselves throughout our careers. We wear this armor whenever we feel challenged or possibly think we don't deserve acknowledgment when it's due.

Our identity is defined by our business titles, ranks, and past accomplishments. Many times we can hold on to the way things have always been done and resist any type of change (even if it's for the better) because the ego wants to protect us from harm and for not being an expert, and from future risk.

But then, some of us have the opposite feeling. We never feel we're good enough or deserve a seat at the table. We come from generations of low self-esteem or years of social awkwardness. We internalize that our opinions and ideas are not worthy like everyone else's.

You may be at either side of this spectrum or somewhere in the middle. But it's essential to notice and decipher whether you show up each day the way you intend and not fall victim to self-betrayal.

In the book *Leadership and Self-Deception* authored by the Arbinger Institute, a company that offers webinars to help businesses improve their team's mindset, motivation, and performance, an act of self-betrayal is described as "an act contrary to what you feel you should do for another."[7]

Without intending to, we commit self-betrayal every day. We usually know the right course of action and trust our gut on the right course of action. But so often in business, when we don't want to do something, it is easier to make excuses—like how new systems or processes are to blame for our lack of motivation or knowledge—rather than take ownership of our story. That is our ego at work.

Here is a story from *Leadership and Self-Deception* that demonstrates how anyone can easily fall into this trap.

Imagine yourself as a father of an infant crying in the middle of the night. You wake up and see it's around 1 a.m. Your exhausted wife doesn't wake up, as she has been up with the baby around the clock for weeks.

In that initial moment you wake up, you know what you should do—get up and tend to the baby so your wife can sleep! But instead, you don't act on your initial thought and you lie there too long listening to the baby wail.

As you stay in bed, you think, "How is she not waking up? I have a long day at work tomorrow, and she will be home, and if I get up, I will be exhausted at work."

Then you think, "She must be faking it!" You get angry at your wife because she is not getting up for the baby.

That moment, right then, is self-betrayal. Your initial thought was the truth and the right action, but instead, you came up with

7 San Francisco: Berrett-Koehler, 2010.

excuses because you didn't actually want to take the action that you knew was the correct one.

To recognize this truth, you need to make space for it. And listen to what it says.

When you react strongly to something or someone, that triggers you to become more alert and try to understand what you are holding on to—and why.

The ego can help and hurt. Even during my childhood, I stayed laser-focused on someday fleeing my situation and doing whatever was necessary to make sure I would never be in that situation again. The drive gave me strength. But at times, it also got in my way.

Growing up, I looked up to the women in my family, my mother and grandmother. My impressions were that they were independent women, and I wanted to be one too. My grandmother didn't marry until her late 30s and divorced in her early 40s at a time when few women lived alone and independently.

My grandmother lived to the beat of her own drummer. She never seemed to care what others thought. One picture of her in scrapbooks always stood out to me. She looked confident, laughing, her blonde curls whisking in the wind on a balcony of a cruise ship, traveling alone at a time when few women dared.

When I was younger, women were just starting to have careers beyond traditional female occupations like nursing and teaching. I was one of the few girls I knew whose mother not only worked but also owned her own business. I was proud of that fact and wanted to be a part of it. I accompanied my mother to trade shows and business networking events as a young teenager. I got to see the inner workings of the business world, and it was exciting! At an early age, I dreamed of being successful, having a thriving career, and living independently and free.

From the time I was a little girl, my mother had put a plaque over my bed that I read every day. It said,

"Don't Tell Your Daughter to Marry a Doctor or a Lawyer, Tell Her to Be One!"

She gave me books to read that depicted women as strong and never needing a man to prove their worth. A few were written by the famous, strong-willed (and at times controversial) Ayn Rand. The author of the classics *The Fountainhead* and *Atlas Shrugged* in the 1940s and 1950s, Rand envisioned a world where strong and independent women would be game-changers in the workplace.

That's when I started to imagine who I would be as a woman. I pictured my life through these books like many of the characters—taking on the world. Whenever there were moments of weakness from the women characters, I was disappointed.

This idea of how my future would look was my ego standing tall and firm to protect me and keep me strong. However, this mindset got in my way because I didn't easily relate to other people my age.

I really screwed up during sorority rush my freshman year in college because of this. When you are part of a sorority rush, you visit each sorority house, and two girls pair up to ask questions. One interview went like this:

"What major are you in?" one of the sorority girls asked me.

"Accounting," I said proudly.

They paused. "At the business school?"

"Yes."

Then one said, "Oh! There are a lot of boys there!"

I quickly responded, "Actually, girls are pretty well represented."

I didn't realize what they were getting at until later—they
were more interested in meeting boys and going on dates. Needless to say, they didn't ask me back. I was *wayyyy* too serious
about school, rather than finding my future husband.

WORKING WITH THE EGO

The ego is a strong and unconscious part of most people,
something we seldom recognize. While it probably offered
protection and helped me survive what I had gone through as
a child, my ego developed into something I needed to learn to
control in my business and personal relationships.

Sometimes, the ego can mislead us if we are not careful
and can keep us in unhealthy situations. I often relied on its
protective armor and mindset against abrasive supervisors and
inappropriate behavior in the workplace. The ego helped me tolerate a lot and keep pushing past bad experiences so that I could
keep my eye on the goals I wanted to accomplish.

The ego showed up in other ways at work too. When I have
felt someone is insulting me or trying to belittle me or my work,
I often have spoken up when others are better at staying quiet.
I have found that sometimes this automatic response can cause
people to misread me and my intentions.

My first lesson on this occurred at my first real job. I quickly learned the reality that a successful career wasn't a matter of only working hard. It was also trying to understand and navigate the interpersonal interactions between my co-workers, my boss, and my staff.

During college, I joined an accounting fraternity. Don't laugh! I know it sounds somewhat nerdy, but I fit in better in this type of fraternity than the social sororities.

The fraternity's focus was to build connections between college students and local accounting firms and corporations. We visited a different large firm each month, learned about their culture, what a career would be like, and met their partners and staff.

At one of the firms, I hit it off with the partner. When it was time to interview for my first job, this person just so happened to be the firm's recruiting partner as well. I was so relieved when I walked into that interview room and saw him sitting there.

However, there was a woman with him that I had never met. She was a senior manager at the firm and threw daggers at me with her eyes from the moment I walked in and throughout the interview. Even so, I got the job—but I knew it wasn't because of her.

As fate would have it, she was my manager for my first assigned audit job—and, of course, future audit assignments that year too. She found every way possible to humiliate me in front of clients. It was a miserable first year of my professional life, to say the least.

In the accounting profession, when people want to leave a firm, the "unspoken" rule is to wait until the busy tax season is over. Otherwise, you risk looking bad and having it follow you and risk future job opportunities. Therefore, there is a wave of accountants who leave firms in the spring and summer. Celebrations and farewell office parties were scheduled many Fridays to wish departing accountants well.

One day, this senior manager announced she was leaving the firm. I thought to myself, *Hallelujah!* Even though she was never nice to me, I decided to still go to her party out of professional courtesy.

As soon as the partners gave her a farewell gift and thanked her for her service, I decided it was time to leave. I walked over to shake her hand and wish her luck. However, she wasn't ready to let me go. Instead, she asked to speak with me in private. She left her party in the large glass conference room and led me into the hallway.

Once we were alone, she said, "Successful women do not look like you." And then a barrage of insults followed, like "you look like a ditz, but are actually smart." She told me that *all* the managers talked about it.

This went on for about 30 minutes, but it felt like hours. I finally left and went to my car, feeling broken and thinking I would have no future with the firm. I went to a local department store the next day and asked for a complete makeover. I didn't want to look like me anymore.

My manager left her legacy internally with me. I believed what she had said and then assumed that everyone thought of me this way. I became very insecure. I showed up to work with my new clothes and makeup and felt miserable trying to be someone I wasn't.

After about two years, I had a review with another manager,

and I blurted out what she had said and my perception that everyone thought of me like that. He sat there in shock and then said no one had ever said that or thought of me like that. On the contrary, they all respected me and ranked me very high. He added that she had never gotten along with many people when she was at the firm.

About 10 years later, I became a partner in another CPA firm and was nominated for an award for the local area. I was so surprised to be put up for this honor. At the awards event, my category was scheduled to be announced first. So, I didn't have the advantage to see how other people accepted their awards and whether you were expected to give a short speech. Since I did not think I had a chance at winning, I didn't prepare any remarks. Well, much to my surprise, I won. They asked me to say a few words when I got on stage. I stood there for a moment, raised the award, and said, "This is for my first manager. She said successful women didn't look like me." I have to say it felt good to say that out loud!

These kinds of false perceptions affect us to the core. Too often we don't take time to understand feedback we receive and whether it's valid or is based on another person's insecurities or personal shortcomings. And, perhaps worst of all, we often don't assess how we carry these stories with us even when we think we are far past an occurrence in our life. Additionally, we don't necessarily always choose our words carefully enough as a supervisor or colleague to ensure no one is walking around with insecurities rather than being lifted up.

Taking a step back to pause before responding and observing myself as a third-party participant has been constant work throughout my career, whether it pertains to how someone treats me or how I react to someone else. Is it them or me? Where is the truth between reality versus perception? I have to constantly ask myself, "What is each person's side?" rather than just my own. This work is never easy. But I find the hardest question to ask myself is "What is my 100 percent responsibility?"

To be brutally honest with myself is tough, but what I have learned along the way, and continue to learn about myself, is worth it.

KNOWING YOURSELF

Everyone needs to realize that each person comes with their own stories, habits, and patterns.

It's not easy to ask ourselves the tough questions and truly embrace the good and the bad. But it's worth it. Knowing yourself will help you keep in Balance to maintain your Bliss. Furthermore, authenticity can help you perform better in business and build stronger relationships at work and at home.

I've learned that in business, as one's power grows, one's willingness to listen shrinks. This is because people think they know more than their employees or feel that seeking feedback will come at a cost. Additionally, people that have not risen to the same ranks often do not give honest feedback to their supervisors for fear of losing their jobs.

So rather than trying to assess ourselves alone, it's vital to bring in these multi-dimensional viewpoints. This way, we don't justify our actions to ourselves but instead understand how our actions affect others and don't align with how we want to show up. (To learn one way to introduce feedback into the workplace, see *Breaking Beliefs* Podcast Spotlight: "The Gift of Feedback," highlighted at the end of this chapter.)

When you see these patterns show up—how you react to others, the feedback you receive during reviews, whether or not you are successful in completing projects on time, how your loved ones respond to you—it's the time to decipher what is perception versus reality.

The first step is to pause and review the situation and decide whether it's them—or you. Where is your ego keeping you from being present and understanding all sides of an experience? What is your responsibility, and have you fulfilled it? Or are you looking to blame the outside? Is the feeling or experience significant enough to hold on to? Or does it make more sense to let it go?

These reality checks are hard, I know. This is where enlisting an executive coach, a therapist, or an independent person you can trust can help provide the outside perspective on your situation you sometimes need. This person is someone with whom you can share and bounce off ideas without having a bias or skin in the game. It's often easier to share our stories with friends or loved ones because most likely they will side with us. And sometimes we just need someone to agree with us—and that is okay, as long as we stay honest with ourselves about each conversation's purpose.

The key to all of this is learning to be more open to third-party feedback without interrupting with our own justifications for what they've observed. Listen to what they say, even if it's difficult to hear. We usually grow the most when we are challenged or feel uncomfortable. Yet, the more information you can gather from yourself and others, the more tools you have to change your mindset and behavior for the better—for you and everyone you interact with.

B³ BREAK

- Exercise 1: A moment of self-reflection

Close your eyes and be still for a few minutes. Allow yourself to be in your truth and take an inventory of your thoughts as an observer, rather than passing judgment on what you are thinking. Being an observer means not judging your thoughts but instead watching them. Allow them to float in and out without getting attached to what you say to yourself. You also can do this simple exercise while walking outside, listening to music, or even driving. The important part is acknowledging your thoughts and being okay with them without judgment.

Repeat this exercise daily to better understand what you carry around internally and how it colors your perception of a situation rather than the reality. Authentic learning about ourselves begins when we no longer push down our feelings because we don't like how they look.

- Exercise 2: Meditating on self-talk

What has helped me decipher between my thoughts, responsibility, and the reality of a situation is a simple 5- or 10-minute meditation where you observe your self-talk. On Byron Katie's website (http://thework.com/en/do-work), she provides four questions to investigate during your meditation:

1. Is it true? (yes or no; if no, skip to no. 3)
2. Can you absolutely know it's true? (yes or no)
3. How do you react? What happens when you believe that thought?
4. Who would you be without that thought?

BREAKING BELIEFS PODCAST SPOTLIGHT
The Gift of Feedback

People tend to be great about giving feedback but not receiving it. But both are necessary. Feedback gives you, your team, and your customers the insight, guidance, and support they need.

Realizing the value (and gifts) of professional feedback was one of the significant pivotal career moments for Jeremy Jones, a partner with the Atlanta-based accounting firm Frazier & Deeter.

Years ago, he recognized that his sometimes-demanding nature negatively impacted his 97-member team, even though he felt that aspect of his personality was often best for the department.

It made him realize that there can be gaps between what you think is best and what others may believe, and that receiving more feedback from his team could help everyone. "But this can be especially hard in leadership, since as you go through the ranks, people don't speak up as much and hesitate to provide feedback," he says. "You start believing your own truths rather than listening to the people around you."

His solution: invite people to review him.

Jones gathered six to eight people he trusted (who had no axes to grind) from several ranks (partners to management to team members) to give him feedback. They shared, with no reservations, everything about him they found good and bad, where he needed to improve, and how to go about it. He repeated the exercise with the entire audit team.

It may be tough to listen to feedback like this, even if it's constructive. Still, having honest, no-filter conversations showed Jones where he excelled and where he fell short.

For instance, he discovered how his struggle with delegation affected everyone. "Everyone said, 'You've got to get rid of some stuff, and you have to trust others.' One person suggested I didn't trust him, which was not true, but it showed me how my actions can affect others." He used this feedback to change his work relationship with this person and develop more trust.

Also, twice a year, Jones invites everyone in his company to offer anonymous upward feedback on the entire operation. They upload their thoughts and comments into an Excel file through a workspace technology program.

And because it is anonymous, people can be open and forthcoming, which offers real constructive feedback. "When people get in that mindset and get in the routine of giving upward feedback, the amount of jewels you can pull out is amazing," says Jones.

To hear the complete interview with Jeremy Jones, visit:

https://www.amyvetter.com/breakingbeliefspodcast/
episode-4-the-gift-of-feedback-with-jeremy-jones.

🔥 MINDFUL MOMENTS

- It is natural to justify our own side of a story rather than look at all sides. To reach the truth often means letting go of our ego, which can be difficult.

- Perception and reality can be hard to distinguish. It is important to look at a story from all sides to come to an understanding of where the truth lies.

- Ego can creep in and create our own unhappiness without us ever realizing it and color our perception that creates our reality. Are there any examples that you thought of where your own ego was getting in the way of your own progress or someone else's?

- When you review your own life, ask yourself: What stories have been passed down and created patterns of behavior in your family that may—or may not—be true? If a story has different sides, how would that change you or the people around you?

- As one's power grows in the workplace, one's willingness to listen usually shrinks. Few people want to give honest feedback to their supervisors. But this lack of honest feedback holds everyone back.

- Be open to third-party feedback. While our friends will likely tell us only what we want to hear, we'll learn more from someone outside our circle, such as a trusted therapist or executive coach.

CHAPTER 4

Never Feeling Good Enough

"Chains of habit are too light to be felt until
they are too heavy to be broken."

—WARREN BUFFETT

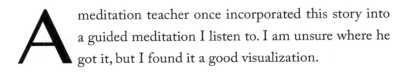

A meditation teacher once incorporated this story into a guided meditation I listen to. I am unsure where he got it, but I found it a good visualization.

Imagine a road you walk down each day with a deep hole at the end of it. Each day you walk down that street and fall into the hole. When you are in the hole, you think to yourself: *I don't want to be here.* But again, you walk down the street the next day and fall into the same hole.

Until one day, you decide to make an effort and practice not walking into the hole.

You may start with knowing that the hole is coming on your walk and pausing before you fall in.

Then maybe you will learn to start walking around it or even taking another street.

With intentional practice, you can make a change. But as with anything you want to accomplish, you have to practice. It's not a fast process, but you must be willing to go on the journey.

Remember the anticipation you felt waiting for your second-grade teacher to hand back your graded paper? Would you get an excellent sticker? A gold star? Or my favorite, a sticker with a watermelon smell?

As adults, we still look for those stickers of acknowledgment. We often seek it from the external sources rather than internally. I have learned over time that it's important to find fulfillment within ourselves because, unlike children, most people overlook your efforts and success unless you point them out. This can sound easier than it is because it takes time to shift how you feel on the inside.

I once had the good fortune to hear Bo Shao, chairman of the Evolve Foundation, at a conference. The Evolve Foundation is dedicated to investing in companies that develop technology to reduce suffering in the world and further develop human consciousness. He began Evolve because he wanted to use his wealth to help others end their suffering by working on their inner self. He believes when we end our own suffering, we can use our newfound freedom and wisdom to help others end theirs as well.

Bo went down this same journey himself. He was born in

China to a poor family. He was exceptionally good at math and later was accepted into Harvard. Bo launched a company upon graduating and later sold it to eBay. His inner journey began when he was 32. At the time, he was one of the wealthiest people in China but found he wasn't happy, or as he described it, he wasn't "free." He often wondered, "Is this just it?" He had financial freedom but still felt empty.

At the conference, he shared his story (you can watch the full video here: https://www.youtube.com/watch?v=I_eFXr4khwE).

In this talk, he told a story that related to his realization of why he was so driven to accomplish. It came down to wanting to please his father. Where he grew up in China, ketchup was considered something for wealthier people, and everyone in his town longed for it. One day, as a child, when he came home from school he saw a bottle of ketchup on the kitchen table. He tried to resist eating it because he knew he would get in trouble, but it was too tempting. When his father came home and realized Bo had eaten it, he couldn't control his rage. The next day, Bo came home again, and there was a new ketchup bottle on the table. Again, as much as he wanted to not get in trouble, he couldn't resist it, but this time asked his father if he could eat it. He was ready to be beaten again for asking, but instead, his father threw his arms around him and said, "You can have as much ketchup as you want!"

Bo was taken aback. He didn't understand the difference in his father's response. His father then told Bo he had won the math competition in Shanghai. He realized in that moment, in order to get the affection, and rewards, he wanted from his father, he needed to continue to achieve at a high level. This pressure to accomplish led him to the success that he had, but also later caused him to break down when he became a parent himself, over not putting that pressure on his children. That's when he went through his own mental wellness journey with therapy to discover what he could do to break those generational patterns so he would not repeat them and affect his children in the same way.

FINDING THE PATH

This kind of learned behavior from our childhood that we carry internally can have effects on us not only personally, but also in the workplace, without us even realizing it. It can cause us to not be authentic in the workplace by protecting ourselves so we don't expose any vulnerabilities we believe we have. We can also end up "wearing" this protective armor at home and around our spouse and family.

In my life, my mom told me stories of how she strived to make my grandfather proud. Similar to Bo's story, without consciously thinking about it, I knew if I did something that she perceived would have made my grandfather proud, I would get her acknowledgment and approval.

I mentioned earlier that my grandfather was a CPA in the 1930s. He came from an immigrant family and became a CPA in hopes of creating a better life for himself and his family. My mother spoke highly of my grandfather and often talked about the "large" firm he had owned. When it was time for my mom to go to college and choose a major, she decided to be an art teacher rather than becoming a CPA. She told me many times that she felt she disappointed her father because she never could take over his CPA practice.

I knew becoming a CPA would make my mom happy and proud. Even though I also was artistically inclined, I went down the CPA path. I dove into this career and never looked back. That is, until I was 32 and made partner at a CPA firm. This firm was a sizable regional company, and it was a huge accomplishment in my career. However, my mother would always take the opportunity to bring up how "large" my grandfather's firm had been, as if to imply that the firm where I made partner somehow was a lesser accomplishment.

Years later, I researched my grandfather's background for a keynote I was developing and found that he had been a solo practitioner. I didn't know what to make of this. Don't get me wrong, I am very proud of what my grandfather accomplished and grateful for the sacrifices he made that benefited future generations of our family. His accomplishments were admirable and didn't need to be embellished by my mother. However, learning that my mom created an untrue story of his accomplishments to imply that mine did not measure up to his took me aback.

Another instance when I learned this lesson with my mom was a conversation she had with my father and repeated to me. My father had not been in my life from the time I was 16 until I was 32. Not having his financial support while growing up, as well as my mom losing her business at the same time when I was in high school, caused me to work multiple jobs to pay my bills and contribute to what the household needed so my brothers and my mom were okay. It was a financial struggle to get to the finish line of college. The day I received my first full-time job offer after college, I was driving my car and had to pull over and cry in relief. The reality that I was going to be able to work just one job and have enough to support myself was overwhelming.

After graduation, I worked in public accounting and then eventually worked for a Fortune 500 corporation doing financial analysis and system implementation. During this time, my mom had a phone call with my father. At that time, my father hadn't been in my life for at least 10 years. She told me that my father asked her what I was doing in my career. She knew I had recently taken a trip to Argentina to help with the company's financial system implementation. But instead of telling him what I really did for a living, she told him that I was in international mergers and acquisitions.

When she repeated this conversation to me, I asked why she said that when that wasn't my job. Her response was that she thought it "sounded better." These were the small whispers I began to notice. I was becoming more aware that it was never enough, no matter what I accomplished.

It took me a long time to realize that no matter what I achieved to get approval, it was only good enough for that moment. Through the internal work I was doing at the time, I realized that I needed to strive for my own success and not accomplish in order to seek her approval.

INNER JOURNEY BEGINS

When I began practicing yoga in my 30s, it was the first time I ever slowed down enough to get in touch with my thoughts and how I felt inside. Until then, I kept my mind and body busy, and I pushed down my emotions and rarely allowed myself to cry or even think, for that matter. I began learning about myself through my yoga practice by getting comfortable listening to my inner thoughts and feelings rather than pushing them down.

As I started learning more about yoga, I found myself getting more and more curious. I wanted to better understand the practice's philosophy and mind-body connection as I got deeper into it, so I decided to train to become a yoga teacher. This was the first time in my life I had done something for myself and not to make someone else proud or try to accomplish a set outcome.

The seven-month training culminated with a week in Costa Rica, where I graduated from the teacher-training program. I was so proud of myself. When I was at the airport on my way home, I felt the desire to call my mom to share the news and how good it felt. Her reply? "You aren't going to tell anyone that you did this, right?"

At that moment, I realized I was just as proud of earning this yoga teacher certificate as I was when I got my CPA license. I told her that this certificate would proudly hang right next to my CPA certificate. It represented a big accomplishment in my life because it was the first time I did something for myself and not for someone else.

After the call ended, I waited to board the plane. I realized how hard I had worked for approval my whole life. Every day I began at zero to earn my mom's approval all over again. And the next day, I had to prove everything again and show her that she should be proud of me. But the question was whether what I was doing was for me—or someone else?

A significant contributor to not feeling I was "enough" comes from generations of the same pattern happening between mother and daughter. An example is how my mom placed an unhealthy importance on beauty because my grandma did that to her. I have a vivid memory when I was in elementary school and my mom took me to the doctor for a wellness visit. The doctor told me I was overweight for my age. I felt utterly embarrassed, and my mom's disappointment that I didn't look as I should for a girl that age stung to my core.

My mom's solution was to limit me to two Oreos every other day so I would eat less sugar. I would prolong eating those Oreos. I separated the sandwich cookies and evenly spread the cream on each side. That way, in my mind, I had four cookies to eat! When it was Oreo day, I awoke with anticipation. On the other days, I just hoped time would go faster so I could have them the next day.

Later, in middle school, my mom repeated to me that my grandma told her that I would eventually be pretty when I was an adult. They had decided that my looks were more "mature" than childlike. In turn, my mom drilled into my head not to focus on my appearance since that wasn't going to help me, but instead accomplish at a high level in music and academics. She didn't want me to do typical "girl" activities, such as dance, modeling, or cheerleading, because she characterized me as a klutz and uncoordinated. Portions of that message were actually helpful. However, I remember growing up looking at other girls and thinking I would never look like them or be allowed to do the fun things they did.

So, I proved my worth through certificates and achievements in my music, education, and career. By the time I had my
first son, I had graduated college, secured my CPA, and finished
my MBA (two weeks before I gave birth). When I decided to
take the insurance exam while on maternity leave, a friend joked
that maybe I should go for a hairdresser certificate next. But the
reality was that I had this fear that I never achieved enough, so
I always strove for the next thing.

I soon realized this tendency to look for approval crossed
over into my work life, too. I became more aware that a common trigger to feel bad about myself was when I believed I had
disappointed someone or felt my work was not appreciated. I
needed to feel positive reinforcement from a manager or team
leader in order to stay motivated and not be too hard on myself.

This was especially evident during my annual reviews. I
could have a stellar review for the most part. Yet when someone pointed out an area for improvement, I focused more on
that comment than anything positive. I became tough on myself
and made it a much more significant issue in my mind and, no
doubt, in my manager's mind, too.

That reaction always brought back the same feeling I had
when I felt I disappointed my parents. Because I utilized the
ego to survive my circumstances, I kept that mindset into my
adulthood, and this same pattern showed up for me repeatedly.
I didn't know how to redefine what this meant, especially how
it influenced my perception of my career and accomplishments.

As I began to work on myself, I acknowledged this emotional
need. I created an expectation for other people without them even
realizing it. They did not view me as I viewed myself. It was much

like Bo's story. I created a shell around myself and had a false sense of what love is and the perception of what I would need to do to have someone love me back or appreciate me in the workplace. I felt I needed to achieve at a high level to earn love or respect.

WHAT WOULD MAKE YOU HAPPY?

Early in my career, as I strove for my next promotion, a close friend asked me, "What could you accomplish at work that would make you happy?"

I found I wasn't able to answer, which was surprising. I felt like I had this deep well internally that I couldn't see the bottom of. What would allow me to fill it up and feel satisfied or even grateful?

This brought me to the realization that it is essential to decipher between the beliefs you listen to in your head or say out loud every day versus those of your soul.

Which comes down to one question: Are your beliefs yours—or someone else's?

These belief systems we have turn into habits, which can be unintended, unintentional, and even unnoticed by us. One approach I have found to help recognize and break free from these kinds of patterns we create comes from an article written by Kaye Ramos in the digital magazine *The Startup* called "How to Break Bad Habits and Set Yourself Up for Success According to Research."

In the article, Ramos writes, "Being open to breaking bad habits puts you on the advantage against most people who deny them. You cannot change something if you can't accept that

Recognizing the Patterns That Are Holding You Back

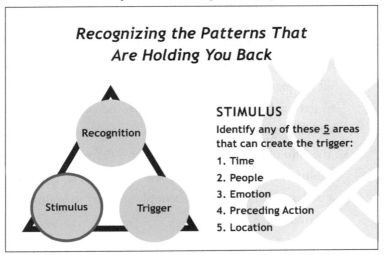

STIMULUS

Identify any of these <u>5</u> areas
that can create the trigger:

1. Time
2. People
3. Emotion
4. Preceding Action
5. Location

something has to change. Small, bad behaviors, when piled up, can have a negative impact in the long run. Your bad habits can create a dent in your productivity."

There are all kinds of "bad habits." Mine was the inability to receive constructive feedback. But no matter what type of habit you want to change or at least minimize—in business or life, or even both—the process is the same. It follows three steps: recognition, trigger, and stimulus. Here is how each one works.

1. The Recognition: Recognizing the pattern of behavior is the first step. For example, I recognize that over time in my career when I encounter a supervisor who is controlling or micromanages, I struggle to get along with them and do my best work. Even though I have learned over time their behavior has nothing to do with me, my pattern is to believe internally they don't think I can do a good enough job or they don't trust me.

2. The Trigger: What causes you to react the way you do or repeat the same behavior? For me, the trigger that sets off the pattern with a controlling manager is when I have to get each step of my work approved and I can't run with a project.

3. The Stimulus: What stimulus creates the triggers for the habitual behavior? Describe these five key areas to uncover a pattern. You can use my example as a way to brainstorm for yourself.

- Time: Is there a particular time of the day you do it?

  - I know my patience with this type of personality is not as good toward late afternoon or after I have put in a lot of hours in a day.

- People: Are there people involved when you do it?

  - I can immediately recognize when I am working with a person who is going to trigger this within me by the way they manage and communicate.

- Emotion: Are you agitated, bored, scared, or something else?

  - My emotions with a controlling manager become impatient and annoyed.

- Preceding Action: What did you do before the stimulus occurred? What action triggered your reaction?

  - When I am dealing with a controlling manager, the preceding action is typically them questioning the little details, rather than seeing the big picture, and slowing progress down.

- Location: Is there a specific place or situation where you always do it?
  - In my example this is in the workplace, but this kind of personality can trigger a response for me anywhere, since I grew up with a mom who was very controlling and micromanaged what I did on a daily basis.

The inner work to break a pattern we recognize is then to become unattached from such a challenging encounter, observe the situation, and then decide on our 100 percent responsibility in the situation and come to a place of compassion rather than fighting back.

One of my favorite interviews was with Dr. Tye and Samantha Moe, who shared their advice on how to take more personal responsibility in how we react to others, both good and bad. (See *Breaking Beliefs* Podcast Spotlight: "Modeling a New Perspective with an Open Heart," highlighted at the end of this chapter.)

So, what if you've developed a bad habit—going to bed too late, procrastinating when knowing you are bumping up against a deadline at work, or maybe even eating a doughnut every morning—how do you go about breaking it? In Ramos's article, she states, "In order to do something different, you have to activate a different part of the brain to override those habitual tendencies, the prefrontal cortex. It keeps track of your current situation and goals, and how they might be different from what they were before."

One way I've learned how to activate my brain in this way is with meditation.

When I started to meditate, I had to train my brain to do it. Meditation has always been something I have struggled with, so I needed to make a commitment to "force" the habit so my brain would eventually naturally want to do it. So, I decided to meditate at the same time each day to begin, starting with just five minutes and building up over time. This helped create the "stimulus" I needed to know unconsciously it was time to meditate.

By repeating this behavior each day at the same time, it started to help me think to do it as soon as I woke up. I also set out a pillow in my room with a blanket. Each day when I woke up and saw the pillow, it created a trigger to sit down and meditate. After developing that consistency, I could use meditation to help clear the thoughts in my brain and observe how I am feeling so I would know how to offset those emotions during the day and create a new pattern I want in my life.

I found it helpful not to overwhelm myself. I gradually increased to meditating for up to 10 minutes in the morning and added a sleep meditation at night. I found that was a reasonable time frame for me. There are days I could go longer, but I don't put pressure on myself about it, or else I lose the benefit. I just take it as it comes and on the days I am distracted and not as still, that gives me insight into what I need to adjust as well.

THE "SIXTH SENSE"

Here's how my meditation practice has helped me break bad habits in the workplace and my personal life. I grew up with what I call a "sixth sense." Since I was never sure if I would please someone or make them angry, I began to pick up other cues on whether I could trust a person or not or predict if a situation was going to turn bad.

When I meet people at work, without realizing it, I quickly size them up and decide whether they are what I consider "real" or have a political agenda. I know people with agendas are a weakness for me because I don't enjoy that part of corporate America and I have never been good at "playing the game." My perception is that they spend more time angling for positioning rather than getting work done. And if you focus more on work than what is going on around you, like I do, it's easy to fall prey and get tangled up in their game.

I have coached others on recognizing tough personalities in the workplace and how to handle the situations they encounter. My advice has helped create success for them in their careers, yet for me, I still struggle.

I pride myself on having an innate sense of human nature from a third-party perspective. I get what others need to do. However, I respond quicker than I would tell someone else to do. I show my emotions when I don't want to and often don't feel good about it later or wish I had handled it differently.

Meditation has helped train my mind, or rather rewire my thoughts where I can. It is a life journey—we never really arrive—but what we learn along the way matters. Through yoga, I studied the concept of non-attachment. In the beginning, I didn't understand it. In essence, the belief is that most humans struggle with attachment, and it is the leading cause of human suffering. So by learning non-attachment, both in good and bad situations, you can work to alleviate your suffering.

Meditation can be a tool that helps you see where your mind attaches to objects, situations, people, and desires. It teaches you how to observe where and when you get attached. As you become more aware of this reaction, the attachment loosens its grip on you over time. (To try a sample meditation, visit https://www.amyvetter.com/breakingbeliefspodcast/episode-73-b3-breaks-a-5-minute-mindfulness-practice.)

Throughout this journey, I have learned to observe my actions and those of others. I can now better decipher my reactions. This is what "disconnecting to connect" is all about. It takes dedication to disconnect and truly connect to the power within ourselves and create the life we desire. You need to pause and review your own thoughts and behavior before responding to others.

This is also a good place in your process to apply my work and life philosophy, the B³ Method—Business, Balance, Bliss—to help maintain your happiness and use your natural "toolbox." (See page 52 in Chapter 2.).

B³ BREAK

Using the pattern model in this chapter, identify a belief system that has turned into a habit or pattern for you. Write down one example that shows up for you at work or personally as a habit that is not something you feel good about, and detail the following:

1. The Recognition: Recognizing the pattern of behavior is the first step.

2. The Trigger: What causes you to react in the way that you do or repeat the same behavior?

3. The Stimulus: What stimulus creates the triggers behind the habitual behavior? Describe these five key areas to uncover a pattern.

   - Time: Is there a particular time of the day you do it?
   - People: Are there people involved when you do it?
   - Emotion: Are you agitated, bored, scared, or something else?
   - Preceding Action: What did you do before the stimulus occurred? What action triggered your reaction?
   - Location: Is there a specific place or situation where you always do it?

BREAKING BELIEFS PODCAST SPOTLIGHT
Modeling a New Perspective with an Open Heart

In their individual businesses, Mad2Glad Parent Coaching & Whole Family Chiropractic, Dr. Tye and Samantha Moe equip parents with information and tools to lead their families with less worry and more ease. Part of their work entails teaching how to be responsible for one's actions and how this affects everyone around us in ways we don't always notice.

Take the simple business mantra of showing up on time. Timeliness is still a struggle for many people, but people often have ready-made excuses for their tardiness. Samantha shares this story:

"Years ago, I had a team member, [and it seemed] like 90 percent of the time, she couldn't find her car keys, or there's traffic, or there's construction outside her place, or her window was frozen shut. It was never her fault, and even though somehow for her, 90 percent of the time she didn't make it on time to our meeting."

The lesson here: Excuses don't lead to change. Instead of owning up to her own poor time management skills, the team member failed to see how her actions affected her and impacted her co-workers. It can hurt to be honest and truthful with ourselves, so we avoid it.

Once you take responsibility, you can implement positive change. Have you ever found yourself being critical of people you just met or don't know well? We probably have all done it at some time, but why? Tye explains that it's part of a self-defense mechanism we create, and it's a way for us to collect ammunition in case a person judges or points out flaws. After all, it's much easier to see faults in others than in ourselves.

The reason for this behavior lies inside. It originates from the negative self-talk we tell ourselves. Am I smart enough? Am I good enough? Do I look okay? Do I say the right thing?

Tye did this too, early in his career. As he says, "Even though I love people and I get along with them well, what I was finding is that my first impression of someone is looking for something wrong with them."

This self-defense was hurting both Tye and everyone around him. He finally had to be honest with his behavior, and only then could he make the necessary change.

Tye did this by flipping his mindset. "As soon as I looked at someone, I would say, 'What's positive about you? Do I like your hair? Do I like your smile? Do I like what you're wearing?'"

Eventually, he expanded this approach to include questions like, What's something in you that I wish I had in me? What's something in you that I'm grateful for? and What's something in you that's the same in me?

"I soon started building these instinct connections," says Tye. "I was leading with love and openness, and something I liked about a person could then shift my energy around them instead."

To hear the complete interview, including their views on how your family and childhood experiences can significantly shape how you communicate and interact with different situations, visit:

https://www.amyvetter.com/breakingbeliefspodcast/episode-6-modeling-a-new-perspective-with-an-open-heart-taking-100-responsibility-with-samantha-moe-and-dr-tye-moe.

🔥 MINDFUL MOMENTS

- As you listen to your inner beliefs, make sure to ask: Are these mine or someone else's? Just because you say something out loud or think it internally and often doesn't mean you originated that belief. It's important to observe beliefs as they arise in us and ask ourselves whether we truly believe that thought.

- Small, bad behaviors, when piled up, can have a negative impact in the long run—in business and in life. No matter what type of habit you want to change, the process follows three steps: recognition, trigger, and stimulus.

- Are there situations at work or in your personal life that you can identify as patterns of behavior? Meditation with practice can help you observe where your mind attaches to objects, situations, people, and desires. The more aware you become of this reaction, without judging yourself, the more the attachment loosens—disconnects—its grip.

- This is what "disconnecting to connect" is all about. It takes dedication to disconnect and truly connect to the power within ourselves and create the life we desire.

CHAPTER 5

The Importance of Community and Compassion

"Once you understand how your body and brain are primed to react in certain situations, you can start to be proactive about how you approach things. You can identify triggers and know how to support yourself and those you love."

—DR. NADINE BURKE HARRIS, AUTHOR OF *THE DEEPEST WELL*

To work through our stories, we must go through the process of letting them go. We appreciate what the experiences have taught us but welcome our next phase. To do this, we have to understand how trauma affects us—and those around us—to create a supportive community that wants only our best as we make this journey of self-reflection. Leaders or team members in business need to understand why someone resists change. It's also necessary for others—a companion, friend, or parent—to understand our behavior and how we may react to external circumstances.

The reason for the way we react to different circumstances or within relationships could be layered beneath our surface. When our ego is threatened, we fight back, and often hard, without even realizing it. When we are afraid we may not be good enough, we resist change even more.

Yet, understanding how our childhood experiences affect our outward responses helps us to better understand ourselves and how to treat the people around us. This helps us learn how to look at each person individually and help them along their own journey as well.

FIND YOUR ACE SCORE

How does this process begin? The first step is to explore your past in more detail. Answering the following questions can help. They may make you uncomfortable but can provide the valuable insight you need as we move through this chapter.

When you were a child, identify any of the following from the list below that applies to you:

- Physical, emotional, or sexual abuse
- Physical or emotional neglect
- Parental mental illness, substance dependence, incarceration
- Parental separation or divorce
- Domestic violence
- Other, or none of the above

This background information is the first step to finding your ACE score. The Adverse Childhood Experiences (ACE) Study was published in 2015 by Dr. Vince Felitti at Kaiser Permanente and Dr. Bob Anda at the Centers for Disease Control and Prevention (CDC). They surveyed approximately 17,500 adults about their history of exposure to "adverse childhood experiences," or ACEs. They correlated these ACE scores against health outcomes and found that 67 percent of respondents had at least one ACE and 12.6 percent had four or more ACEs.

They found that there was an association between ACE scores and health outcomes. The higher the score, the worse the health outcome. For a score of 4 or more, the risk of obstructive pulmonary disease and hepatitis was 2.5 times that of someone with a score of zero. For depression, it was 4.5 times more likely, and suicide was 12 times more likely.

Looking closer at the results, the researchers found that early exposure to adversity affects children's brains and bodies. The experiences can influence pleasure control, impulse control, and executive function (skills like planning, focused attention, remembering instructions, and juggling multiple tasks). They also can affect the brain's fear and response centers. Physically, the immune and hormonal systems can be damaged.

(You can find more information on ACE, the study, and its findings at the CDC webpage: www.cdc.gov/violenceprevention/aces/about.html.)

In her TED Talk, Nadine Burke Harris, author of *The Deepest Well*, discussed a randomized controlled trial published in 2015 of kids in institutionalized care (who had been removed from their home) and kids placed in homes with high-quality caregiving.[8] The children had MRIs at age two and then again at age eight. The results found that the kids who had been put into high-quality nurturing caregiving homes had different brain structures than those who remained in institutionalized care. The study also showed that high-quality nurturing caregiving—which included safe, stable, nurturing relationships—may actually change the structure of children's brains. It did not necessarily have to be care from a biological parent—it could be a strong bond with any person who provided unconditional love and support.

The message here: Bad stuff can happen, but a nurturing environment can change you. And you also can nurture others and change their outward reactions.

But it all begins with recognizing what is going on inside. Getting your own ACE score is the first step in the right direction, and many websites offer ACE score quizzes. (You can find resources at amyvetter.com.)

The next step is identifying your overactive stress response and which situations activate it. For me, the overactive stress response that I brought into adulthood from my childhood was putting up a wall of protection when new people enter my life. This happens at work and at home. This "wall" helps me to make sure that no one can hurt or disappoint me. My past experiences in my childhood affected my "flight or fight" response as I grew up and into adulthood. I trained myself as a child and teenager to not be scared when someone hurt me and instead get tougher

---

8 https://www.ted.com/talks/nadine_burke_harris_how_childhood_trauma_affects_health_across_a_lifetime

each time, so I didn't show weakness and I could prove to myself that I didn't need anyone to make me feel okay.

Growing up, my father spent a lot of time working out. We had an exercise room in the basement, and he made a beeline to it as soon as he got home from work. As he benched and lifted weights in the basement, the booming roar of clanging metal and grunts vibrated up through the vents in the house. Everyone could hear him yelling through each rep and set. I had to be ready at a moment's notice for his call for me to come down and spot him on the bench press. I was expected to bolt down the stairs whenever I heard the call "AAAMMMMEEEE" when he was ready for me to come down. I always wondered how I would actually help him if the bar fell on him, since I was five-foot-two and weighed about 115 pounds, which was almost as much weight as he was benching. Because I was so scared of that happening, I tried my hardest to push that thought out of my mind.

As a child, I remember thinking that he was the best-looking father. I was always so proud of his muscular frame—except when I was at the wrong end of his strength when he was angry. This same strength also created fear when I had girlfriends over to my house. There was no way to be distracted from his grunts and screams from the basement workout room no matter where you were in the house. When he emerged upstairs after a workout, his muscles were extra pumped up, he was saturated in sweat, and his adrenaline was sky-high. My girlfriends' eyes grew bigger and rounder with fear when he walked toward us, and they would giggle nervously. I made light of the awkwardness and tried to make it seem normal so they would not be scared and would want to come back to my house.

When he was angry, my father used these same muscles as a scare tactic. He pointed his finger powerfully close to my nose and would yell in my face. It always scared me. But after years of being terrified, one night when I was in bed I finally made the conscious decision that the next time he did it, I would not react or show fear.

When my father realized he wasn't getting my usual response from his finger-pointing, he escalated to becoming more physical. When this would happen, I did my best to stay focused and not let him see me scared. I was determined to stay strong and not let him think he was breaking me.

However, the truth was I would cry at night in my room and couldn't sleep. All I could visualize was how his eyes would look at me with pure hatred during those outbursts of anger. But on the outside, I stopped responding. I lost my natural fight-or-flight response to what others would consider dangerous situations and refused to flee.

Even emotionally, I learned to turn off my expectations of the love I so badly wanted from him. Sometimes I saw him in the family room watching TV and I wanted to be close to him. But he would keep one leg out sideways across the rest of the couch so he could sit there without anyone bothering him. I remember when I was about 10 years old, and he picked me up after summer day camp. We were walking to his car and I had a moment of feeling overwhelmed with how much I loved him. I threw my arms around him right then, but he quickly pulled my arms away and scolded me for doing that in public. I walked the rest of the way with tears filling my eyes, but I was careful to not show I was crying.

As I entered high school, there began to be a shift for me internally that I was not worthy of love. I would look in the mirror and think I was ugly. This mindset led to many relationships with boyfriends where I accepted bad treatment because I felt that is what I deserved.

I desperately longed for my parents to love me the way I wanted. Even though at that point I considered them my best friends, looked up to them, and valued their opinions above all others, inside I struggled. I visited my friends' houses and watched the easy, stress-free relationship they had with their parents. Their parents were loving and they did not seem bothered if their children asked for something or needed anything, and their household was not rigid with endless rules.

I innately knew I didn't have that. In my head, I wanted to protect my parents because of the trauma they endured with their own parents that they repeatedly told me about. Throughout everything, all I focused on and cared about was protecting my brothers from the trauma they were experiencing from our parents, and my mother and father never doubting my loyalty to them. I never acknowledged my own trauma because I had to be strong to get through my life and accomplish what I wanted, all while protecting everyone else.

After college I left the city where I'd grown up. My mother wanted to move south, so I moved with her. When I decided to move back to where I grew up, 14 years later, I renewed relationships with some childhood friends. When I saw their parents again as an adult, there was a floodgate of condolences. Everyone commented on how sorry they always felt for me because of the situation with my parents. When I went back to my childhood doctor, he talked about my parents and said that, of course I have stress-related issues because "anyone with parents like yours would."

I was shocked that all of these adults saw through the good face I always put on and the outward appearance of what I thought looked like a loving family. No one was fooled but me. I had tricked myself into believing what I had wanted and carried it with me for far too long.

We can pretend our past experiences don't affect us in the present, but we need to be honest. We can choose to blame the previous generations for our current actions today, or we can take responsibility as an adult and identify how we got to the present moment. I made the conscious choice as an adult to not allow myself to use the past, as my parents did, as a scapegoat for my own behavior at work or home. Instead, I had to acknowledge that the trauma occurred and make the intentional decision to not repeat the behavior with my children, family, friends, and co-workers.

By taking a deeper look into what has occurred in my life, I now know when I act out and can be honest with myself— even when I don't like what I see in my reflection. Those are the internal messages and moments of awareness that tell me to pause, step back, assess, and take action. I have to decide to choose to be different and not follow the path of the generations before—and actively ignore that path. Choosing to consciously decide how I want to show up in life and interact with the people I work with or the people I care most about is a continuous journey. I am always learning, I am never finished, and I just try to live each day the best I can.

TAKING A PAUSE

When you observe yourself acting in a way that isn't productive or doesn't contribute in a positive way to those around you, that is your message to take a pause. When you notice this behavior, ask yourself the following:

- What feelings or emotions is a current situation bringing up for you?
- Is there is a change at work, or do you have an interpersonal conflict, technology disruption, or business process reorganization, that is causing you to react a certain way? What may be the underlying cause?
- If you are struggling with a relationship (work or personal), what could be causing your reaction to the other person?
- What is the course of action you would prefer to take?
- What can you learn about yourself?

Rather than focusing on the other person's behavior, or blaming your own past trauma, make an honest assessment of how you can shift this unwanted energy and try another approach. Sometimes this means pausing and being still. You observe the feelings that come up and recognize whether you have felt those feelings before and what the circumstances were. Then you can dive into whether this is your intended reaction—or whether you would prefer to react differently.

What would that look like? Here are some steps you can take. Journaling the answers could be a great way to work through it.

1. Pause and check in with what is going on in the current moment. What happened and how do you feel about it?

2. Allow yourself to absorb these feelings and sit with them without distractions. Try not to check your phone or look at email. Just allow yourself to remain still.

3. Observe these feelings and whether they are related to past issues or beliefs you have about yourself. Ask yourself whether these thoughts or beliefs are true. How would you rather respond and what would that look like?

4. Create an intention, a mantra, or a word that can provide the energy you want to create rather than the negative thought or belief. Repeat that intention silently as needed or write it down and refer to it throughout your day. Notice whether a small shift in your approach changes the experience.

Next, adopt some evidence-based interventions shown to help manage and counter toxic stress, which I discuss in more detail in my book *Business, Balance & Bliss*. For example:

- Regular exercise or some movement at least 30 minutes a day

- Good sleep hygiene that provides you with a way to relax before bed so you can sleep through the night (i.e., no caffeine, food, television, social media, or work at least an hour before bedtime)

- Mindfulness meditation either a few minutes throughout the day or at regular times, such as after you wake up or before bedtime

- Eating clean foods rather than processed
- Not using artificial ways to mask emotions or feelings, such as alcohol or drugs
- Therapy when needed

Getting over my beliefs that "therapy is for the weak" and "yoga is silly" was the beginning of my personal journey to break free from my internal stories. Through my internal work, I realized those beliefs had been placed in my mind and were not my own. During the time in my life when I began both therapy and yoga, I finally gave myself permission to tap into my inner thoughts and feelings and allow myself to feel them.

When I began therapy, I also discovered yoga during this newfound awareness. I silently cried through many yoga classes. The yoga mat was where my body could release the emotions. Instead of ignoring them or pushing them down, for the first time, I allowed myself to tap into that internal awareness and knowledge of how I was feeling. I could now take the time to clear the emotions and do what was necessary for myself and those around me.

But we can't always do it alone, or feel like we need to.

In our lives, it's essential to know the people whom we can trust. Typically, this is a small and select group, and we need to recognize who those people are. How do we take care of, protect, and nurture those relationships above all else? That also is part of our work—to allow other people to support us.

Safe, stable, and nurturing relationships are healing. As the ACE study showed, they are not just nice to have but can change our biology. We have the opportunity to create this at work and home, so people feel supported and safe. However, if we have never had that type of leadership or role model in our life, we need to seek out an example to follow.

HAVING THE TOUGH CONVERSATIONS

I met my lifelong best friend in the third grade. She was like a sister. Our families were friends for a while when we were little. Our fathers were quite similar at the time, as they both were charismatic and outspoken. We both grew up sometimes in fear of our fathers.

By the time I was 16, my father was no longer in my life after my parents finalized their divorce. However, my best friend's parents did stay married and over time her relationship with her father improved. When she was in college, my best friend didn't have much contact with her father because of the experiences between them while she was growing up. Yet, after she finished graduate school, she began working with her father in their family business.

It wasn't long before she was honest with her father about how he could trigger emotions from their past by the way he spoke to her or interacted with her at work. Before she admitted this to him, her father never realized he had that effect on her. He took her feelings to heart, and after that conversation, he made real change. They were more open with each other about what triggered them both when those emotions from the past would arise, and they were committed to improving the future of their relationship.

After college, my best friend and I lost touch for a while. When we finally reconnected, and I saw her with her parents now as an adult, I noticed how they had changed and took an active part in her life and her children's. I now had a real-life example of what true "unconditional love" looked like, and I noticed the security and safety she felt by having them be a part of her life. It was different from the direction my family went, with everyone dispersed and living separate lives.

My friend's parents demonstrated the importance of community and nurturing in the present moment. We are never too old to need nurturing. It is possible to recover from toxic relationships when both parties are open to change and listen to one another and make the effort. It is never easy, but the result is that, as my friend's case shows, the wounds of their past were healed because they demonstrated they were committed to make the necessary changes because they loved one another.

It is never too late to gain self-awareness if you love another person enough to really hear them. Because my friend's father was willing to change and she was ready to share her feelings, their relationship got a second chance. I believe both would say it is one of the most important decisions of their lives.

This type of conversation isn't a one-time event, nor is it easy. It takes a team effort for both people to speak up when triggered by old patterns and internal stories. This level of awareness and commitment to take responsibility and action has allowed them to heal. It not only benefited my friend and her parents but their grandchildren, too. Because their present was course-corrected, and both made real change, past trauma was overcome and now is a distant memory.

Sometimes when we are in conflict with someone we love, we forget that we are on the same side and there is no "winning." To heal, it takes loving the other person enough to hear them and make the necessary adjustments.

BUILDING A COMMUNITY OF SUPPORT

As I went through my own transformation, I knew I wanted to break the patterns of my past and ensure my children's lives would be different from my upbringing. However, before seeing my best friend's family, I didn't know what that looked like. They gave me a vision of the kind of parent I wanted to be for my children and future grandchildren.

There was no reason to focus on it, dwell on it, or talk about it. Because living life in the present moment, with unconditional love, was all that mattered. Unfortunately, my family didn't function that way. Instead, they wanted to wallow in the past rather than do the work to make actual change, so I had to make the hard decision to break from it.

It takes work to build a community of support. One day, when I was in intense therapy, I had this moment where I felt what I describe as the "pane of glass" disappear between myself and my toddler children. I wasn't aware it was there, and they probably didn't notice, but something inside me innately knew something was wrong. It was this: I always felt guilty putting them first before my parents and brothers.

But no more. My life changed from that moment forward. I decided to protect my children from being harmed by the so-called ghosts of past generations. As an adult with my own authentic beliefs, I had to take a stand to stop the cycle. It was going to end with me, to the best of my ability.

My therapist always described two types of people: one that can expand their heart to allow more people in, and one that has a set number of spaces for people in their heart, and they feel threatened by anyone who comes in from the outside, whether it be in their personal or work lives.

To overcome our generational beliefs coming into our present day, we need a community that will support us as we change. Sometimes, we don't realize or recognize who these people are in our lives.

Growing up, I had another best friend named Luke. No matter how depressed I got because of my family and when I felt my world was falling apart, he always showed up for me. When I was in my most profound depression at age 17 and didn't want to get out of bed for high school, he would force me to get out of the house. His love was unconditional. I remember vividly one of our last conversations when we were seniors. We went out for ice cream, and he asked me how I pictured my life, and I said, "I am going to be successful and have a *big* corner office with windows."

He said that sounded lonely. I told him I wouldn't be.

I then asked him what he pictured, and he said, "to live hard because I am going to die young. I'm going to get on my motorcycle and leave for Florida."

I was taken aback and asked him why he thought he would die young. Luke said that there was a history of early death for men in his family, and he had a feeling it would happen to him.

Luke died of a brain tumor when he was 29. And he was right. I did feel lonely in a corner office. That is when I learned that you can't do this alone. You need a community, and he was my first teacher without even knowing it.

THE CIRCLE OF TRUST

Years later, at a work dinner, my co-workers and I decided to not talk about work and instead play "two truths, one lie." It's played like this: Each person tells two facts about themselves (the truths) and one lie. Everyone then tries to decide which is the lie.

We learned a lot about each other. One person had a powerful story of leaving his family at a young age. After a series of traumatic experiences with his brother and parents, he knew he had to estrange himself from his family to create a new life for himself. He spoke about how hard it was to not allow them to get close to his current family, and from that moment he had to run his life differently. He had to be vigilant about those patterns and behaviors from his former family being separated from his current one. He called it protecting his "circle of trust."

When we define the members of our circle, it's just as important to identify the people who are not supportive and don't serve our own growth as knowing who the supporting people are.

My circle of trust includes two girlfriends that have been in my life since I was young. I can tell them anything and know I am safe. They remind me that I'm not crazy and validate my feelings when no one else does—and vice versa. They make sure I always know they love me and support me, whether with hugs physically or through their words and actions.

Because each of us carries these stories that affect us

emotionally, when we are in leadership positions in the workplace, it's essential to be sensitive to others' stories. When we are honest about what we personally bring into the workplace, it's easier for us to nurture our teams, so they know we care.

To create trust at work, it's imperative to create an environment where people can trust their leaders and each other. A concept that demonstrates this is called Radical Candor™ (www.radicalcandor.com). It's the ability to directly challenge and show you care personally at the same time. Radical Candor can help you and all your co-workers build the trusting relationships you all need.

Creating a relationship that is bidirectional, rather than top-down, is vital. When your team trusts you, you can help push them past their own fears and insecurities to accomplish what they desire. It allows you as a leader and co-worker to be open with your team when they are off track or out of scope on a project in real time, rather than waiting for a too-late annual review. With this approach, they know you care and want to help them improve and are not trying to trip them up. These relationships can be open enough to provide valuable feedback to improve your leadership skills. Putting yourself in a position where others can see and hear what you can offer can make you feel vulnerable. But this is the heart of being a Connected Leader and provides real professional growth. This means letting your team know when things are not going great—and not always showing that everything is perfect.

I once had a project that was different from any that my team had done before. We had nothing to reference or iterate on, and it all was done from scratch. The first round did not go well. However, when nothing was working out at that moment of weakness, I brought everyone together to openly discuss the problem. But I also challenged them so we wouldn't give up.

We talked about what did not go well and what needed to improve. We also noted what already worked and should be continued. I was open with them that if I lead and they are somewhat uncomfortable, we are not innovating, and I am not doing my job.

In the end, we created something better together because I allowed everyone, me included, to be vulnerable and not pretend that everything was terrific. We aired emotions and solved problems. Learning from each other what doesn't work the first time helps us improve the second time and avoid the same mistakes.

ATTRACTION OF NON-ATTACHMENT

Through the teachings of yoga, I have learned about non-attachment and not having expectations. These two factors create much of the suffering and pain we experience in our lives. In the beginning, I didn't completely understand it: How could it be possible to have no expectations of another person? For some yogis to do this, they choose a life where they remove themselves from society. I thought it may be easier to practice non-attachment and no expectation that way. But for everyone who can't do this, we have to constantly experience other people, their behaviors, and how that affects us internally.

Through my own journey, I have defined this philosophy as learning how to limit the power and response I have to another person's feelings, emotions, and behaviors. I recognize that they are on their own journey, and I try not to attach my emotion to theirs. Instead, I learn to observe my actions and others' actions as a third party. What is my 100 percent responsibility, and what is theirs? What can I accept in my life, and what will I decide to not accept? Where do I choose to set boundaries and release myself from the chains of guilt when I don't do what someone else wants me to?

This should be practiced in business, too. We encounter challenging personalities and unexpected economic or business forces we cannot control. So ask yourself, "How can I become unattached from the circumstance and be the observer? How can I not feed into it and take it personally?" I have to decide my responsibility and what journey others are on to arrive at a place of compassion. Sometimes, this means giving myself time before responding to a situation and playing out scenarios before deciding the best course of action.

One thing I have learned from my life experiences is how to keep my head down during chaos. I know how to stick it out during hard times and give myself the time to correct the course. If I keep my vision on the ultimate long-term outcome, the present situations are something I can detach from.

There is no way to predict whether the decisions we make are the best ones, but as long as we know we did our best and made the best choice based on what we understood, then that's all we can hope for. This is why defining our personal purpose, as we will do in Chapter 6, can provide a North Star to help you navigate your way back when you wander off your path.

It's also important to become unattached from perfection and wanting to please everyone. Surrounding ourselves with nurturing relationships can release us from this guilt and help us realize we are imperfect human beings, as is everyone around us. This way, we define what we can and cannot tolerate, and it provides guidance in how to deal with whatever comes our way.

We create this community of support at work, so we feel nurtured and cared for. This may sound touchy-feely, but as the ACE study pointed out, most people around you at work and in life have experienced some sort of trauma.

It's possible to find ways of developing more compassion for others and see them as humans, not just co-workers. We don't necessarily have to tell each other our deepest, darkest secrets. However, knowing that two out of three of us have experienced trauma is excellent knowledge to have as we respond to each other. How could this information change the way we interact, solve problems, or create more empathy in how we see people respond in meetings or one-on-one?

Additionally, take the proper time to develop your own team and community of support. Executive coaches, sponsors, and mentors are invaluable in giving the feedback you need. (See *Breaking Beliefs* Podcast Spotlight: "Looking for 'Me' in Others: Utilizing the Power of Mentors to Help You Get to the Next Level," highlighted at the end of this chapter.) Be sure to look for people who won't necessarily tell you what you want to hear.

How can they help you stretch to become better because of the relationship, make you feel safe, and ensure your conversations are protected? They have your best interests at heart.

Don't necessarily wait for your company to formalize a program around this. If this is important, reach out to people you think can help you. Nurture and develop these relationships and find ways to give back to them.

I found that giving back opens up another community of support. Rather than always focusing on our own journey, we need to serve others. In college, I found a way to give and receive as a volunteer at a center for grieving children. Here, children were mourning siblings or parents who had died from disease, sudden accident, suicide, or murder. Each night was dedicated to a specific type of loss, and similar-aged children who experienced that loss were brought together in support groups.

At the time, I am not sure I understood why I was so drawn to serve there. I had found out about the center from a charity event I attended. I immediately felt a strong pull to see how I could help these vulnerable children. Once I committed, the center put me through a group facilitator course.

I realized that this was not a sad place, but the opposite. The center was the only safe place these kids could go where others like them understood what they were going through. They felt heard. They didn't feel rushed to "get better." Everyone understood. It was their circle of trust.

B³ BREAK

Create your circle of trust for work and personally. Make a list of these individuals, why they belong, what specific skills they provide, and how they match up to your needs. If you notice gaps, develop a strategy as to whom you could target.

BREAKING BELIEFS PODCAST SPOTLIGHT

Looking for "Me" in Others: Utilizing the Power of Mentors to Help You Get to the Next Level

Madeline Pratt, CEO and founder of Womxn Talk Money, has built her career around the intersection between technology, sales enablement, and channel development. As a business development leader and creative consultant, she works with thousands of accounting firms from around the globe to assist them with technology, branding, and sales.

After spending eight years leading sales for tech companies in the accounting space, Pratt focused her attention on helping firms grow. She offers online education programs and community groups through firm forums and founded Womxn Talk Money, which is designed to help firms innovate.

Along the way, she has discovered the value of mentorships—from seeking out a mentor to being one herself.

Here are a few of her lessons.

Mentors come in many forms. A mentor can be someone we don't know but look up to. For instance, growing up as an aspiring athlete, Pratt's first mentor was the soccer star Mia Hamm. Hamm was her ideal of success, a strong female role model, and someone she could relate to.

Find people to help with long-term vision. Mentors can help with short-term goals, but find individuals who can provide the traits and guidance you need to achieve that long-term vision.

Mentors don't have to be business-related. Inspiration comes in many forms. For instance, Pratt's mother was a mentor who gave her the freedom to have a creative lifestyle and the support that she could do anything.

Revisit past mentors. Pratt has found extra value in maintaining longtime relationships. You never know when you may need a former mentor's advice. Pratt has gone back to her high school physics teacher on occasion and utilized that relationship to shift her career. To maintain those connections, we have to nurture relationships along the way and never forget people as we move forward.

Mentorships can have future payoffs. You never know what skills or knowledge you may need down the road. Cultivating mentors from different areas with various skill sets can help you become more well-rounded and even be a source of future insight. Case in point: Pratt developed a mentor relationship early in her career at a financial software company where she learned the ropes of the emerging field of cloud technology. The experience became invaluable when she had the opportunity to launch an Australian technology company's United States team.

To hear the complete interview, visit:

https://www.amyvetter.com/breakingbeliefspodcast/episode-24-looking-for-me-in-others-utilizing-the-power-of-mentors-to-help-you-get-to-the-next-level-with-madeline-pratt.

☸ MINDFUL MOMENTS

- We all carry experiences from our past into our present, but we have a choice. We can blame the previous generations, or we can take responsibility as an adult and identify how we got to the present moment.

- Realize that most of the people around us have experienced some level of trauma in their life, as revealed in the ACE Study. It is important as a Connected Leader to recognize that and work with each person individually to uncover what they need to break past any fears and find success in the workplace.

- It is possible to recover from toxic relationships when both parties are open to change, listen to one another, and make the effort going forward. Coming up with an agreement and how to let one another know what triggers them is important so both parties can heal and move forward.

- Creating a relationship that's bidirectional, rather than top-down, is vital for a healthy work environment. When your team trusts you, you can help push them past their own fears and insecurities because they know you want to help them improve and are not trying to trip them up.

- Putting yourself in a position where others can see and hear what you offer can make you feel vulnerable. But this provides real professional growth, and it's at the heart of being a Connected Leader.

CHAPTER 6

The Intuitive Mind versus the Rational Mind

"The intuitive mind is a sacred gift, and the rational mind is a faithful servant. We have created a society that honors the servant and has forgotten the gift."

—ALBERT EINSTEIN

This profound and transformational work to understand ourselves is a lifelong journey. We may think we have it all figured out, and then life throws us a sharp-breaking curveball. But this winding, ever-changing path is the real journey—to study our mind, body, and soul.

I often feel I am in an internal boxing match between what I intuitively know and feel versus what I want to rationally believe and force myself to think.

Sometimes this struggle is so deeply ingrained that we never even question it. Who put these ideas there? Are they ours? Or did someone else tell us to believe a particular thought?

Ingrained beliefs are hard to overcome but always should be questioned.

Throughout my life I have always been considered a klutz. I trip when I walk, I hit my head on things constantly (even though I am only five-foot-two), and I spill drinks, food, you name it on myself in the most inopportune times.

I heard my parents call me a klutz all the time. There were many things I asked to do when I was little, and one of them was to learn to dance. My parents wouldn't sign me up because they thought I was too uncoordinated to be a good dancer.

These messages that became my own beliefs have always made me worry that I am going to trip, hit my head, or spill something, because everyone around me always predicts it. When I wanted to try out for the dance team in high school, I held myself back because I could hear the messages that I would never be good at it and would fail.

All of these messages can be said jokingly to me, but because I know people are watching for it, it immediately makes me self-conscious, and then more than likely I create their truth because I am thinking it too.

Until I started yoga. I never thought I would be good at yoga because for so long I considered that I could never move my body that way. I remember that when I began it was the first time I pushed past the thoughts and didn't care if I would be good at it. I instead was more in tune with my intuitive mind that it was something I needed in my life, and it felt good. I remember looking around at some other people in the class and having the thought that I would never be able to do what they could do, but it didn't matter. I just wanted to be there.

More than eighteen years into the yoga journey, I broke that belief system along the way. I not only can do what those other people could do, I can get into poses I never thought would be possible for me. It took practice and also required releasing those beliefs about myself that were not mine, but were someone else's.

This has been a lesson for me in other ways too. For example, how to be careful with my words with others. Words matter. I believe that if you have a passion for something, it's worth trying. It's important we don't set an expectation for ourselves that we have to be the best at everything. If we find joy in it, it's worth doing. Even more important, we shouldn't get in the way of others in their pursuits. If we ever do that to another person, we should pause and try to understand our actions and then make the adjustment so we can offer the support they need.

FINDING SELF-DISCOVERY

Many of us aren't able to break free from our rational mind. We go through our lives believing what the outside world tells us to believe or what we want to believe. However, we have our truth talking back to us if we choose to listen.

This internal conflict happens not just in our personal life, but also in our work life. When I speak at conferences about digital transformation and organizational change, I ask the audience what they are most concerned about regarding their future career. The top answers are typically—

- Becoming obsolete
- Losing my job
- Keeping up with all the changes

When we don't stop, pause, and listen to what is going on internally, that is when we begin acting in fear or in ways that prevent us from living the life we desire. Instead, we are more influenced by external forces: other people, artificial substances, images we want to emulate, belief systems of others. We don't realize our self-worth or trust what our intuitive mind is trying to tell us.

Self-discovery can be one of the more courageous acts someone can do for themselves. You may think taking time for self-discovery sounds selfish; however, when you help yourself, you help the people around you, too.

One way to begin this journey is to better understand our own personal purpose. Once we do that, then we can create that awareness for ourselves. Rather than assuming all the feelings, opinions, and actions are our own, we decide to question how we think, speak, and act. Gaining a better perspective of what formed those beliefs we hold internally is an essential step in asking who we are and what has influenced us along the way.

When we define our own personal purpose, all the other decisions we make in life, at work, and at home become easier. Once we define it, we can use it as a guiding light. (See *Breaking Beliefs* Podcast Spotlight: "You Can Be the Same Person at Work and Home," highlighted at the end of this chapter.)

We align personal or business decisions with our individual purpose to help measure whether we are moving in the right direction. Even if it means we are stagnant, we are consciously choosing to stay right where we are because we understand the bigger picture and how it will fulfill our personal purpose in life in the long run. When we do this, it's essential that we also take accountability for our choices, whether they turn out good or bad. We own our choices and are aligned to our overall personal purpose.

If we find our choices are out of alignment with who we are, we can then change course on our path because we have created a heightened awareness and are more in tune with ourselves. It's an excellent exercise to take the time and do this for yourself. Begin by drafting a personal purpose statement (see B^3 Break on page 136).

For me, this personal purpose has remained the same throughout my career. It has taken on a different meaning over the years; even when I have made career or family life changes, I have used this as my guiding principle. If I can't make a positive change for the people around me, then my personal purpose can't be served. I then need to find a way to adjust or pivot without losing the experience and expertise that I have built over my lifetime.

When we tune into our intuitive mind and create this personal purpose statement, it allows us to bring our authentic self to everything we do, whether in our work or personal life. We align to our inner soul to ensure we are "real" wherever we show up. That means being the same no matter the situation and bringing our best attributes and qualities to everything we do. We give ourselves the freedom to take the "mask" off and feel more fulfilled by what we do and whom we choose to spend our lives with.

HONEST ASSESSMENTS

When you strive to become a Connected Leader in the work-place, it is vital to use this awareness of yourself. Sometimes you have to get past your rational mind and tap into your intuitive mind, especially when trying to surround yourself with the right people and being empathetic to people that you don't naturally align to.

I have found that it helps me to not hire people who think exactly like me or have the same strengths and weaknesses. If my entire team thinks alike, it is hard to grow. It may be nice for everyone to nod and agree with every idea, but in the end, it doesn't create a better result. By being more self-aware of my strengths and where my gaps are, I can make sure my teams are more well-rounded so they can be good at the things I fall short at or don't enjoy.

When we go through self-assessment, we need to be aware of our good skills, admit our weak ones, and be honest about which tasks we do and don't enjoy doing. It's essential to fill team roles with people who can fill in the gaps and enjoy the work they are doing.

I once had an employee who was my right-hand person, and I relied on him to do tasks I didn't enjoy and, frankly, wasn't good at. Our department took a personality test at this particular company, and this employee's profile came out the complete opposite of mine. He later shared how concerned he was that I may not like that we were so different.

I was surprised he felt that way, and I told him that is exactly how it should be. My goals were to hire people who address my weaknesses, so I had the time to focus more on my strengths.

I knew I would do a better job as a leader by working with someone who wasn't just like me and could challenge me on the details that I didn't necessarily naturally pay attention to.

To be a Connected Leader, we need to be comfortable hearing differing opinions and viewpoints. We also need to be comfortable admitting when we aren't good at something and not try to be everything to everyone. If we attempt to do everyone's job, we do a disservice to the people around us by not giving them the space to learn and grow. When we are grounded in our own personal purpose and live it, this becomes more comfortable as we go along.

This is not always a quick fix. It is a lifelong journey because life is constantly changing, new circumstances arise without our control, and we need to be open enough to realize it. The goal here is to be more aware of ourselves, make the minor changes and adjustments in life when we need them, acknowledge where we are at that moment, and then get ourselves back on track.

Sometimes, to grow means letting go of some part of ourselves. The important part is letting go of the past. What may have worked before may not be the best course of action now, and we have to be open to studying ourselves and block out the outside noise of expectations and belief systems that don't align with our own. This can feel confusing, but it's actually a good sign when it happens. When we get in tune with our intuitive mind and think that we are off-balance, our internal teacher tells us a shift needs to occur. It is up to us to decide what to do with that information.

Do we resist it, or are we open to what may come to be?

We have developed belief systems that helped us survive and

navigate through life transitions. We can be thankful for that, rather than feeling we need to hang on for dear life or blame our current circumstances on the past. We may just need to create a deeper understanding of that experience to better understand ourselves and keep growing to our next best self.

When uncontrollable or unpredictable circumstances cause changes at work or in our personal lives, it is up to us to observe and gain an understanding that the ego holds on to our old self for protection; it is what we know. That is where the fear lies—telling us we may not be good enough. Instead, when we identify our own personal purpose, we create self-worth and a personal mission. Everyone has something unique to offer, and if we make time for self-discovery, we can find it.

When experiences in the past have hurt us, we may use these past stories as an excuse to fire up our rational mind to declare justifiable reasons why life is going the way it is today. However, when we listen to our intuitive minds, we can decide instead to pause and become more curious and more honest with ourselves when faced with life's ups and downs. We realize we are responsible for our own behavior, and we become ready for our next phase by pushing past the fear and breaking free from that old protective shell that worked in the past. If we choose to not break through and do this work, it's hard to discover that new part of ourselves to expose to the world. It is a constantly evolving process and takes time. But it's worth it if we want to continue to evolve and create a better life for ourselves and the people we care about.

I am not saying this work is easy; I have been there. Letting ourselves go through the emotions to allow ourselves to heal is the work. Everyone finds their way of doing it, but for me, it was necessary to go through the pain of my past stories to break through and get in touch with my own mind, my own beliefs, so I could design my present and future in a new light.

This evolution has its own pace, and yours may take time, but stick to it. There is no magic to it or amount of time that it takes, you will just know when you feel a shift, even little ones along the way. By creating that internal awareness, you will know when you need to make your next subsequent adjustment and then step back and listen to what your intuitive mind is trying to tell you along the way.

This excerpt from *The Four Agreements* by Don Miguel Ruiz[9] always helped me understand to not rush it or force the process, but instead take it as it comes.

There was a man who wanted to transcend his suffering, so he went to a Buddhist Temple to find a Master to help him. He went to the Master and asked, "Master, if I meditate four hours a day, how long will it take me to transcend?"

The Master looked at him and said, "If you meditate for four hours a day, perhaps you will transcend in ten years."

Thinking he could do better, the man then said, "Oh, Master, what if I meditate eight hours a day, how long will it take me to transcend?"

The Master looked at him and said, "If you meditate eight hours a day, perhaps you will transcend in twenty years."

"But why will it take me longer if I meditate more?" the man asked.

---

9 San Rafael, CA: Amber-Allen, 1997.

The Master replied, "You are not here to sacrifice your joy or your life. You are here to live, to be happy, and to love. If you can do your best in two hours of meditation, but you spend eight hours instead, you will only grow tired, miss the point, and you won't enjoy your life. Do your best, and perhaps you will learn that no matter how long you meditate, you can live, love, and be happy."

B³ BREAK

To create your personal purpose statement, first reflect on the following:

- Define your "Why": Why do you do what you do? What drives your passions and gives you fulfillment?
- Describe your passions and the values you hold true. Do you align with them? Are any out of alignment with who you are?
- Gain clarity as you set goals in your life, whether in your career or personal life, to ensure they align with your individual purpose.
- Take control and decide how you want your story to go, rather than letting someone else control it or letting life just happen.
- Simplify your direction. To be balanced, you will either align with your purpose or not. Decipher what you should stop doing, continue doing, and begin doing.

Gaining this kind of insight can help you create a well-defined statement. When drafting your personal purpose statement, follow this formula:

The value you create + who you're creating it for = the expected outcome.

For example, my personal purpose is: "I want to help people find fulfillment not only in the work they do, but also personally so they are able to create the life they desire, maintain their happiness, and be intentional about the energy they want to create for themselves and those around them."

BREAKING BELIEFS PODCAST SPOTLIGHT
You Can Be the Same Person at Work and Home

People strive for work-life balance to provide boundaries between their two worlds. While there are many advantages to this division, the leadership qualities you offer at home also can benefit the workplace. In fact, at times, you should be the same person in both places, according to James DeLeo, the leading partner of the business consulting and accounting firm Gray, Gray & Gray. For example:

Family First. DeLeo and his team incorporate a "family first" culture in the company. "For us, culture has always been critical and our primary focus because at the end of the day, the only thing that we have as a firm is the people," he says. "That is what makes up our firm and many others. We're constantly monitoring culture."

How does he do that? One way is to host multiple town hall meetings of about a dozen people to discuss specific themes (similar to a family dining table discussion).

Here is an example: "We do hundreds of employee benefit plan audits. At one point in time, one of our auditors raised their hand and said, 'I am working on employee benefit plan audit after employee benefit plan audit. What I notice is everybody's employer match is higher than us. I'm curious as to why that is.'

"The candid answer to that person was, 'I have no idea.' We looked, and sure enough, we were below market. It was addressed appropriately by the person. By the same token, we were equally as upfront that, as the managing partner, I wasn't even aware. My point to the whole firm was this affects everybody. This is partners and employees. This is something that needed to be addressed and was addressed."

Summer Fridays. Another way they embrace family-first culture is Summer Fridays. People can take off Fridays during the often slower summer months. But it's not about one person being off, but an entire department. This way, you can really invest in your personal time without having to worry about a co-worker or manager trying to call or email. Everyone enjoys the same benefit. The company even continued it through COVID-19. The feedback from his staff has been supportive.

"There was a time where we were the only ones doing it," says DeLeo. "That time has since passed. A couple of folks have said, 'that was a cutting-edge idea. We'd like you to come up with more of them.'"

To hear more about DeLeo and his views on business, visit:

https://www.amyvetter.com/breakingbeliefspodcast/
episode-90-you-can-be-the-same-person-at-work-and-at-
home-with-james-deleo.

🪷 MINDFUL MOMENTS

- Self-discovery can be one of the most courageous acts someone can do for themselves. It's not selfish, because when you help yourself, you help the people around you.

- One way to begin a journey of self-discovery is to better understand our own personal purpose.

- If we find our choices are out of alignment with who we are, we can change course by tuning in to our intuitive mind and aligning with our inner soul to ensure we are "real" wherever we show up.

- Sometimes in order to grow we need to let go of some part of ourselves. This can feel confusing, but it's actually a good sign: It's our internal teacher telling us a shift needs to occur. It's up to us to decide what to do with that information.

CHAPTER 7

Coming into Awareness

"Study, when it is developed to the highest degree, brings one close
to higher forces that promote understanding of the most complex."

—YOGA SUTRA 2.44, PATANJALI

E veryone walks around with internal stories. Many look at
their own life story and traumas and wonder, "Why did
this happen to me?"

However, the truth about life is that whether we have good
or bad experiences, the lessons we learn teach us that we are not
unique. Would it have been better if our experiences happened
to someone else? What makes us different? Here is a fable that
has been told for years and years that offers some insight into
this concept.

A massive storm came into a town. An emergency warning went out ordering everyone to evacuate immediately. A

pastor heard the alarm and decided to stay, saying to himself, "God will save me."

The neighbors came by his house and asked him to leave in their car, but the man declined, saying, "God will save me."

As the water rose, a man paddled by in a canoe and called to him, "Come into my canoe!" But the man again said, "No thanks, God will save me."

The floodwaters became higher, and the man retreated to the second floor. A police motorboat came by and saw him and said, "We will rescue you!" But the man refused, saying, "God will save me!"

The floodwaters rose higher, and the man climbed to his rooftop. A helicopter spotted him and came to his rescue. But again, the man refused: "God will save me!"

Shortly after, the man drowned. When in Heaven, the man stood before God and asked, "Why didn't You come and save me?"

God said, "Son, I sent you a warning. I sent you a car. I sent you a canoe. I sent you a motorboat. I sent you a helicopter. What more were you looking for?"

This fable demonstrates how we can't always wait for someone else to save us. Instead, choosing to be responsible for our actions and mindful of how we affect others is an essential step toward awareness. Whatever experiences we have had—whether our fault or someone else's—we can only control our reaction and our actions toward those around us.

This is what mindfulness is all about. It is the awareness of how we affect the outside world, take responsibility for our actions, and learn to have more compassion and acceptance of others. When we notice a learned behavior from a parent or sibling emerge from us, it's our choice as to how we react to it. We can blame our own behavior on them or choose to step back, assess, and do the necessary work to break the pattern.

But just like everything else in life, the desire to improve this mindset takes constant practice and intention.

THE WORD *DHARMA*

In Hinduism, *dharma* is the behaviors considered to be in accord with the order that makes life and the universe possible, including duties, rights, laws, conduct, virtues, and the "right way of living."

Dharma is about getting to the root of suffering so we can get to the end of it, which involves going deep into yourself to find where the drama disappears. Mindfulness practices can help create this type of awareness by going below the surface of anger, sadness, or despair.

Part of that process is forgiving ourselves and those around us to find peace and move forward.

It took me a long time to understand this concept because, frankly, my mom didn't believe in it. I grew up with generations of family members cutting each other out of their lives. I have many cousins, aunts, and uncles, but I don't know any of them, and I wouldn't recognize them if we ever met.

My family's pattern is not turning back once someone has "crossed" you. Because of my mom's experiences growing up with her mother, she harbored much pain and sadness. Whenever the topic of forgiveness came up, she would brush it aside. She didn't believe in forgiveness, so in turn, neither did I.

After my parents divorced when I was 16, my father was no longer in my life. My mother continued to harbor a great deal of anger toward him. When memories of my father came up, and I didn't know how to deal with the sadness of how much I missed him, my mom always returned to her teaching of not forgiving the people who harmed us. Even though it never felt right internally to not forgive, at the same time it also made me feel stronger to push down the pain.

I grew up in the Jewish religion. One of the year's highest holy days in the Jewish religion is Yom Kippur, the "Day of Atonement." During Yom Kippur services, you stand and read aloud a list of sins and say out loud that you forgive yourself and others who have done those acts.

Whenever it was time to say one of the lines where you forgive the people that have harmed you, my mom would put her hand over the passage and cover it in my prayer book so I wouldn't read it aloud. We both stood silent, not reading while the rest of the congregation did. I was so nervous each year, anticipating that line being read and knowing I would need to stand silent. I always felt that I was doing something against God by not reading it, which disturbed me. I never showed her that it bothered me because I didn't know better at the time and wanted to follow what made my mother comfortable.

Later, when I began my own self-discovery and was in therapy and beginning yoga, I did a lot of research and soul searching. During the heaviest time of my therapy, I read *Eat Pray Love* by Elizabeth Gilbert, and there was a passage that forever changed *my* beliefs about forgiveness.

In her book, Gilbert is suffering from a divorce and looking for a resolution to her pain. She travels to India, lives in
an ashram, and tells of her experience during a meditation
one night on a rooftop. She was given a piece of paper with a
guided meditation written on it. She read it that evening and
part of it said,

- With all your heart, let go.

- With all your heart, forgive him, forgive yourself, and
  let him go.

- Let your intention be freedom from useless suffering,
  then let go.

- When the karma of a relationship is done, only love
  remains. It's safe. Let go.

- When your past has passed from you, at last, let go.

- Then climb down and begin the rest of your life. With
  great joy.[10]

After reading this passage, she goes into deep meditation.
She realizes she may never talk to her ex-husband and give or
receive forgiveness because of how their relationship ended.

She instead invited the memory of him to silently join her
in her meditation that evening on the rooftop. She then stepped
back into her mind and became the observer of herself and
the memory of her ex-husband. She watched how she and her
ex-husband could forgive each other, so they could create space
for what comes next in their lives.

---

10 New York: Penguin/Riverhead, 2007, Kindle chapter 60.

After reading this passage, I imagined my father and me on this roof. I finally let go of the anger and disappointment over what I had hoped our relationship would be. I gained a new perspective of the realities of each of my parents, how their relationship affected each other's behaviors, and how it impacted me. I gained a new perception of my mother's role and realized I needed to find a way to break from that control she had over me.

There wasn't a day between the ages of 16 to 32 that I didn't think of my father and feel pain for losing him in my life. Soon after I read this life-changing book passage, I took the steps toward healing. I drove to my father's workplace, bringing a blank sheet of paper and a pen.

I sat outside his office building, staring up at the office space he inhabited, and just took in everything. Then I began to write my father a letter. I didn't plan the words or edit them as I wrote. I just wrote what came through me at that moment. I wrote about my struggle to understand his actions from the time I was young to the present day. I now understood some circumstances that contributed to his behavior that I wasn't aware of at the time. I wrote that I never would understand his or my mother's actions, but I chose to forgive, so I could release the pain of the past and move ahead. I ended the letter by saying I didn't expect an answer. This was just something I needed to do for my peace and well-being. Then I walked into his building and left the letter in his mailbox.

My father called me later, and we talked. And for a while afterward, we met for coffee or lunch. Our conversations were mainly on the surface, like visiting an old friend. However, a family incident caused us to speak more frequently years later. During one of those talks, my father finally apologized.

He took responsibility for the pain he caused my brothers and me, with no excuses. He said that both he and my mom were damaged people and they had not been "qualified" to have children together.

I didn't realize how badly I needed to hear him say, "I'm sorry." I could finally get some relief from the pain. There now was an understanding for his part in the trauma my brothers and I endured. His acknowledgment helped me remove the barriers needed for true forgiveness.

And that was forgiveness. Now let me be clear. I did not forgive my father's abuse. But I forgave him for being human, and this allowed me to create space so I no longer harbored this pain in my life or defined myself by it. I accepted that I would never get what I needed from my parents or have them create the relationships I had dreamed of with my children as well. However, by going through this challenging process, I could release myself from the past and make a positive change for myself, not repeat the pattern, and ensure my children would have a different life than me.

And since then, every year at Yom Kippur, I have read that passage on forgiveness loud and confidently. Even with memories welling up of my mom covering the passage and tears in my eyes, I now make the choice to forgive.

This doesn't mean I never feel disappointed or sad about how my family's relationships played out, but I no longer harbor anger. We have each created separate lives, some of us still in touch, but not what I had wished or hoped for as a family. I had always wanted my parents to be involved grandparents where my kids could find another safe place to land beyond myself and their father. I came to the hard realization that after an entire lifetime of trying to keep everyone together and happy, for me to create peace for myself, I can instead choose to love my family from afar.

I accept this so I won't get trapped in the cycle of anger and trauma and instead can create a better experience for those around me. Sometimes it is hard to believe how our lives have turned out. This was the last outcome that I ever wanted. Sometimes, I wake up in the night and, like a bad dream, realize that this is just life's reality. I never imagined not sharing my everyday life with my parents. But I have learned to accept my current circumstances, and they have too.

It was important to me to not bring drama into the lives of my loved ones, my circle of trust. I needed to break from the patterns and stories of the previous generations so the current and future ones could thrive. I want to love my parents, but unfortunately, I can only do so if I don't allow them to hurt me. I know they love me, but they have an unconscious tendency to hurt me, even when they don't intend to. I can't change them, so I have to determine what is acceptable for my health and that of my family and love them at arm's length. This was not an easy choice, and I certainly don't recommend it unless you have exhausted all options. However, we need to reach the correct conclusions for ourselves with non-judgment.

THE THREE MS

Part of what has helped me separate and not judge myself is what I call the three Ms: Meditation, Mindfulness, and Mantras.

When our intuition or "gut" informs us that we have betrayed ourselves in how we react at work or home, we have tapped into our authentic selves. This makes us more aware of how we feel and impact others. We can ignore these feelings and push them down, but eventually, they arise and come out in ways that we can't control. When we choose to not control our energy and put that out in the world, the pattern and the cycle in our life continues.

We all have bad days: days we wish we hadn't said something that we did, or took actions that we wish we hadn't. We wish we could have been more mindful in those moments and made better decisions. But our work, our commitment, is to forgive ourselves, learn from it, and do better next time.

Creating that kind of awareness creates the energy that surrounds you and that you put out toward others. Recognizing when that energy shifts internally is key to making the necessary adjustments we need in our lives, so we show up every day how we want to, and not let the day happen to us. We can use these internal tools whenever they are needed, becoming aware of when we need to pivot.

Because of my yoga practice, this awareness for me revolves around the three Ms. These practices help us tap into our energy, embrace how we feel in the moment, and make the shift intentionally to create our desired outcome. When I teach people who want to become yoga teachers, I explain that the three Ms collectively are our natural human "toolbox" that we can tap into when we need it. They help us to be still and inform us how to better understand ourselves and interact with the world around us.

I have turned to meditation to help train my mind to be more present and aware of my feelings so that I don't repeat the generational behavior patterns I don't want in my life. Additionally, it allows me to understand what I bring into a conversation or an experience that may color my emotions or perception of another person. Meditation helps me when I feel off, so rather than responding to those feelings right away, I can take the time to explore them and understand why I feel that way. I cannot confuse my emotion attached to one person or experience with another situation.

Mindfulness teaches us that there is goodness and purpose in everyone and everything around us. It's natural to focus on the negative automatically. We often spend time talking about negative stories or gossiping about our friends, family, and co-workers. It is hard for our minds to separate the negative and instead look for the positive and have gratitude for our experiences. Mindfulness is also a practice that can benefit the workplace and there are many ways to do it. (See *Breaking Beliefs* Podcast Spotlight: "Take Mindfulness Off the Cushion: Begin with Compassion," highlighted at the end of this chapter.)

Mantras—repeating a word, phrase, or sound—help with concentration during meditation and creating the energy we desire. They also can teach us to be more aware of the positivity and purpose in every living being, for instance, by reciting a daily mantra out loud or to yourself, such as "see the best in others," or "make someone smile today." Other similar positive messages can be a constant reminder of the type of energy you want to emit. When life gets away from you and you feel negative emotions, you recite a mantra, adjust your outlook, and reflow your energy intentionally in the right direction.

When we shift our energy and focus on positive thoughts, we are not defined by failures or bad experiences. We don't relive the past over and over. We also don't define another person we are with by past stories or gossip. Instead, with mindfulness, we are present in the moment. We choose to live for today; we view another person with compassion and acceptance for their situation in this moment. Negative feelings don't trap us, nor do our past stories.

As adults, it seems we have fewer and fewer moments of celebration, and we have to make them happen. So, look up and look around, see the positive, and celebrate!

It is essential to celebrate ourselves and each other, especially our co-workers. These are the moments people remember. It can be a thank-you for a job well done, an acknowledgment of a milestone accomplished, or just a smile to let someone know you see and appreciate them. Make it a daily practice, and you'll be amazed at the energy it creates for everyone, including you.

B³ BREAK

One way to practice daily mindfulness is to focus on gratitude. It's a way to train your brain to focus on positive emotions instead of negative ones.

continued

Here is an exercise you can try.

Write down five things you are grateful for in your life. It could be something ongoing or something new. The items don't have to be "deep" in meaning. For instance, they could be the simple moments of life that you appreciate, such as a slice of your favorite pie, the good weather, an unexpected compliment from a stranger, you were able to make someone smile, the sun came out, your gratitude for your friends, family members, and co-workers.

If work-related, focus on small achievements worthy of celebration, such as hitting milestones and completing deadlines along the way on a long-term project, or completing priority items on your to-do list that you had set for the day.

Keep track of the list and go back to it from time to time as needed when you have rough days or are battling past emotions.

BREAKING BELIEFS PODCAST SPOTLIGHT
Take Mindfulness Off the Cushion:
Begin with Compassion

Scott Shute was head of mindfulness and compassion programs at LinkedIn for several years. He has studied and practiced mindfulness and wisdom teachings since he was 13 and has taught them since college. Along the way, he has explored the human potential to help employees become the best version of themselves.

LinkedIn's mindfulness programs strive to build employee capabilities around resilience, self-awareness, and a growth mindset. The company expands its employees' abilities and service capacity with its compassion programs.

Whether you want to adopt more mindfulness in your life or integrate it into your workplace, here are a few strategies that Shute recommends to get you going.

Create space. Many companies create space for practicing mindfulness. It could be a group meditation room or a quiet or prayer room where people can practice as they wish. Create your personal space at home.

Make it actionable. Mindfulness is more than spending time in quiet reflection and meditation. Try to apply it in everyday life with gratitude. For instance, LinkedIn begins each team meeting with everyone sharing something they are grateful for. Sometimes it's personal, and sometimes it's professional. "When you begin with gratitude, everybody begins from a different position," says Shute. "It opens their heart, and it gets them more open. Starting with gratitude, it gets people in a more creative spot and builds more openness."

Embrace small amounts. We don't always have the time for formal mindfulness practice. Sometimes you have to fit it in where you can. A small amount of mindfulness is always better than none at all. When you have a crunched schedule, focus on reserving a few moments here and there for mindfulness. LinkedIn schedules meetings to conclude at 25 and 55 past the hour, which gives people five minutes to get ready for the meeting or the next one. "It gives people a little bit of breathing room in between meetings," says Shute. They can use that time for mindfulness and take a moment to ground themselves.

To hear the full interview with Scott Shute, visit:

https://www.amyvetter.com/breakingbeliefspodcast/
episode-68-take-mindfulness-off-the-cushion-begin-with-
compassion-with-scott-shute.

❦ MINDFUL MOMENTS

- When our intuition or "gut" informs us that we have betrayed ourselves in how we react at work or home, we have tapped into our authentic selves. We can ignore these feelings and push them down, but eventually, they arise and come out in ways we can't always control.

- We all have bad days when we wish we hadn't said or done something. But our work, our commitment, is to forgive ourselves, learn from it, and do better next time.

- Becoming aware of an inward shift helps us make the pivot we need in our dealings with others.

- It is essential to celebrate ourselves and each other, especially our co-workers. It can be a thank-you for a job well done, an acknowledgment of a milestone accomplished, or just a smile to let someone know you see and appreciate them. Make it a daily practice, and you'll be amazed at the energy it creates for everyone, including you.

CHAPTER 8

Trust the Process to Break the Patterns

"Achieving the life of your dreams and experiencing continuous
personal evolution means commitment to the long game."

—ANTHONY MOORE

According to Jack Kornfield, a renowned meditation and mindfulness teacher, you can change your genetics and even your DNA within eight weeks of training your mind in compassion and mindfulness.[11] The key to breaking your patterns and creating the life you desire, according to Kornfield, is consistency and developing the behaviors you want to foster in life.

No matter what it is in life we work toward, we need to create awareness of our actions and how we show up for ourselves

---

11 See his website: https://jackkornfield.com.

and the people around us. I have found there are good days and ones that could be better, but trusting the process even when it doesn't feel good helps us to keep our eye on what we dream of, rather than giving up along the way.

I believe we all have a "unique soul." No two people are alike. When we try to be something we aren't, it doesn't feel authentic, and it doesn't "stick." This doesn't mean you need to change who you are, but instead embrace and accept yourself and learn how to shift your energy to be a better person for yourself and everyone in your life.

Of course, life does not stay stagnant as you go through the process. There are many starts and stops and ups and downs along the way. It takes hard work and dedication to make this level of change. For me, this has meant making rapid sprints over many years to create the changes I needed. It has taken a lot of work so I could show up for my family and in the workplace in an intentional way.

Have I ultimately succeeded? It's a constant work in progress. But I am better at noticing when I get off track than when I began. What I have learned to do is be more aware, step back, and realize when I need to adjust.

If we want to continue to grow and evolve, our version of ourselves must also evolve—whether it's in business, at home, or elsewhere.

CREATE A PERSONAL PLAN

Many of us are used to creating business goals and plans for each year, but we also need to create an annual *personal* plan to help keep us on track. Define what you need to work on, why, and how you believe it benefits you. Then develop a plan with intentions to make sure it happens. Remember that it is never a one-time fix. Once you have achieved a plan's goal, you have to work on it every day to make it a habit so it comes naturally.

It's hard not to get upset at the small things each day. But try to stay focused on the bigger picture. One of the lessons I taught my children is this: "The power of who we are on the inside is what we do when no one is looking."

To get through the trauma of my high school years, I would muster the inner strength to get up each morning and repeat to myself the mantra, "I am going to be successful one day."

I don't know where that inspiration came from, but it got me through the dreadful feeling of helplessness that followed me throughout the day. I needed something to focus on that I could control until the day came when I knew no one could control me.

I remember attending my college freshman orientation by myself. My mom did not attend, and my dad wasn't in my life at the time.

My most vivid memory is walking up a steep street to the orientation at the student center. When I reached the top, I found myself looking down at the school's football stadium. It was so immense that it took my breath away. As I gazed across the empty seats and the field, I was impacted by what it represented—a symbol of hard work, purpose, and what would help me get to my "success one day."

I took a deep breath and walked into the student center. I was finally going to begin college—and the rest of my life. This brought me one step closer toward success and control over my finances and choices, so no one could ever take anything away from me. At the orientation, all the other freshmen came with their parents. I immediately put up my protection shield and said to myself, "I'll be okay." But, looking back, I felt sad to be there alone, and I had no one to ask for advice or to get help understanding how college worked.

Fast-forward many years later to my son being invited to a special orientation at my former university. As I accompanied him and we walked on that same street up toward the student center, there was the football stadium I had looked down upon years before.

I stopped and asked him to stand where I had once stood and took a picture of him. He had no idea how important that picture was to me. Here was my son who earned his way here, and unlike me, he was always supported and loved along the way. The photo was an emblem of how I had broken the patterns of previous generations.

Instead, I was with him during his orientation, so he was not alone. As he began his journey to fulfill his dreams, tears welled in my eyes, and my heart filled with unconditional love.

At that moment, I realized this was all I had ever really wanted. I fought my way out of my situation, never really knowing what was on the other side, but here it was. I could finally answer my friend's question from so long ago, which I was unable to answer at the time, when she asked, "What will make you happy?" Seeing my children thrive and live out their drives and feeling supported—that is what brings me happiness.

But the work continues. I have to constantly remind myself

not to crave what I'm not supposed to have or live a life of wondering "what could have been." I now live in the present and do my best to devote more time to appreciating what I have instead of focusing on what I don't.

I have continued to return to therapists when I feel off. I use yoga techniques and exercise to work out my internal feelings and emotions, so I don't harbor them and unintentionally behave in a way I don't intend. I also understand that we all need help at times and there is nothing wrong with admitting that and reaching out for assistance. (See *Breakings Beliefs* Podcast Spotlight: "Ask for Help: You Can't Do It Alone," highlighted at the end of this chapter.)

It's up to us to create more positive experiences and shift what we need to shift so we don't hold on to our negative stories that take us away from our work and how we collaborate with each other to create our own experience.

It took me a long time to write this book because I wanted to provide lessons that I hope will help others. I wasn't sure how my story would help because I didn't get the outcome with my family that I had desired my whole life.

I still miss my family and will always love them, but I cannot control the journeys they choose to take. The ability to love someone should be separate from the desire to change someone you love. Your opportunity is to decide what you can or cannot accept from others in your life, no matter how much you care for them, so that you protect *your* circle of trust.

I once listened to a podcast with Tara Westover, author of *Educated*, where Oprah Winfrey interviewed her, and she said the following words that resonated with me: "You can love someone and still choose to say goodbye to them. You can miss a person every day and still be glad that they are no longer your life. We do love a disservice when we make it about control—you give love for free, not to change someone else."[12]

I can't promise that you will get the desired result you want in your life with the people you care about the most. But what you can define is what you will allow in your life and how you want to interact with the world around you, your family and friends, and the people you work with.

When writing this book, I reconnected with the therapist I saw in my 30s when I began my transition story. He was the one who always encouraged me to write my story to help others in similar circumstances. When I saw him, I explained my same dilemma that my ending is not a perfect ending like in most books.

In his sage-like way, he said, "But . . . your ending is your beginning."

So, I hope I have inspired your new beginning, or inspired you to stay on the path if you have already begun the process, to be a better person for yourself and those around you.

---

12   https://super-soul.simplecast.com/episodes/tara-westover-educated-fFrvfnPN

B³ BREAK

One of the lessons I've learned from my yoga practice is the set of guidelines called *Purusharthas*, which are yoga's four aims of life. They are considered the blueprint for human fulfillment. Purusha is defined as the "soul," and Artha is "the ability" or "for the purpose of." Put them together, and you get "for the purpose of the soul."

The Purusharthas ask you to take the broadest view of your life. Are you managing the day-to-day that supports your inner work and the work you put out externally? The Purusharthas consist of four pillars:

- Dharma (duty): How you serve your family, community, yourself, and your obligations and ethics
- Artha (prosperity): How you maintain livelihood and health
- Kama (pleasure): How you create joy in your life and the world; your greatest pleasures and strongest desires
- Moksha (freedom): How you find freedom from areas in your life that feel restricted or burdened

Here is a self-inquiry exercise based on the Purusharthas. The aim is to help identify whether you are internally balanced and, if not, how to make adjustments. When answering the following, reflect on your activities at work and personally, then journal your responses.

Duty: Think about your activities over the past week: How did you serve your family? Your community? Yourself? What were your obligations? Ethical tests you faced?

Prosperity: What did you do this week for the sake of your livelihood? What did you do to maintain your health? Did you have any concerns?

continued

Pleasure: What actions did you take solely to create more joy in your life and world? What was your greatest satisfaction? What were your strongest desires? Were you able to realize them?

Freedom: Record the activities you engaged in, for instance, yoga, meditation, prayer, chanting, spiritual reading, and self-inquiry. Did you find a feeling of freedom? Which areas of your life feel restricted or burdened? What do you need to do to liberate yourself?

BREAKING BELIEFS PODCAST SPOTLIGHT
Ask for Help: You Can't Do It Alone

Like most ambitious businesspeople, Melisa Galasso, founder and CEO of Galasso Learning Solutions—offering continuing education courses for CPAs—has struggled with perfectionism. She did everything (or thought she needed to). But the reality is that we all need help.

Galasso realized (often the hard way) that we need to build a support network and team to create the best success. This is true in business and in one's personal life. It really does take a village.

If you struggle with asking for help (or even admitting you need it), here are some tips Galasso has learned.

Asking for help is not a sign of weakness. You don't know everything, you are not good at everything, and you don't have the time for everything. Admitting this is the first step to relinquishing control, but never associate needing help with weakness or failure. It's the opposite, and it shows strength and wisdom.

Join a group (or two). Getting involved with other

like-mind people, such as women's businesses and networking groups, can help you find support. After all, you are not alone in this struggle, and others either are looking for the same assistance or have gone through it themselves. You may even be able to offer some guidance. And when you help others, they help you, and it becomes a multiplier.

Consider a career coach. A third-party observer can look at your career, life, and work and see things you don't. An unbiased perspective can be enlightening and alter your trajectory. Galasso says that her experience with a coach helped her change her thought process and think differently.

Learn to delegate (and start small). Do you spend too much time and energy on tasks that keep you away from doing what you do best? Examine where you devote your attention and ask yourself if you are the best person to do it. Galasso did this and realized that she didn't (and shouldn't) be booking her own travel or generating invoices.

Once she outsourced those tasks, she had more time to apply her skills where they were most needed. This can carry over to your home life too. "I hired someone to come and change my cat litter because I didn't like to do it," says Galasso about the delegating lessons she learned from her business. "I'm like, I can find someone to do this cheaper than me."

To hear the complete interview, visit:

https://www.amyvetter.com/breakingbeliefspodcast/episode-18-ask-for-help-you-cant-do-it-alone-with-melisa-galasso.

☙ MINDFUL MOMENTS

- Many of us are used to creating annual business goals and plans, but we also need to create an annual *personal* plan for what we need to work on, why, and how we believe it will benefit us. This is an ongoing process: Once you have achieved a plan's goal, you have to work on maintaining that goal every day to make it a habit so it comes naturally.

- Remember, we all need help at times and there is nothing wrong with admitting that and reaching out for assistance—whether it be from a therapist, yoga class, a meditation session, or even a trusted friend.

- You can't—and shouldn't want to—change others. But you *can* choose what to allow in your life and how you want to interact with the world around you, your family and friends, and the people you work with.

- I hope the ending of this book serves as a beginning for you on your journey to disconnect from what's not working and connect to what moves you forward.

Acknowledgments

I would like to acknowledge all the people who have contributed to this book, either with their stories and suggestions or with their support in getting this message out to people who are in need of change in their lives. This book has been an idea that began more than 15 years ago at a therapy appointment with Jay Asher. Without him, my journey would not have been possible. He supported me during the worst moments and gave me the strength to keep pushing through and not try to go around it, and to feel the emotions so I could heal. He planted the seed for this book, and because of that I wrote down stories over the years as they came up for me so that one day I could share them.

When I decided to launch my keynote speaking career, I thought I would start with this book; however, once I started writing I shifted course and wrote my first book, *Business, Balance & Bliss*, instead. Through that book and related keynotes, I gained the confidence to share more and more of my personal stories. Which led me to decide to sign up for a speaker training to hone my speaking skills further.

There I met Michael Port. I spoke to him briefly at an event prior to attending the training. He asked me what keynote I was bringing to training. I told him I was bringing my existing one for *Business, Balance & Bliss* to further refine. That's when the next challenge came. He asked me, "Is there anything new you have wanted to write, since you are taking on this training opportunity and will have the experts around you to help?" I told him how I had these stories written in my phone that I had not had the courage to write as a book yet. So, he suggested I put together the keynote script first, test out the stories and see what resonates, and if it worked out the way I hoped, then write the book. Then he left it for me to decide. Well, once that idea was in my head, I could no longer put off walking this path to share these stories that I hope will help others.

This journey began with the biggest gift that I have ever received: becoming a mom to my sons, Jagger and Austin. Without becoming a mother, I probably wouldn't have awakened to the change that needed to happen in my life. The love and trust we have together as a family I never knew existed. They have been supportive of me writing this book, reading it themselves to give feedback, and providing the encouragement to keep going, even when at many times writing this book was challenging. I love them more than I could have ever imagined loving anyone. They are my heart and they are my purpose to keep working hard to be as good a person as I can be every day.

Then there are my girlfriends, Stephanie Cable and Jenna McHugh, who have served as my confidants and mutual support throughout my life. They have been my family of choice and more like sisters than friends. They have been my cheerleaders to support me in getting this message into the world and supported me from childhood into adulthood as I worked through the emotional work I needed to do to heal.

I would like to thank Michael and Arlene Cable for providing me an example to follow of the type of family I aspire to have. Your example has not only helped me and my children, but future generations as well.

I would also like to give thanks to Luthor Whitehead, who passed away when he was 29 years old. He was the first person in my life who understood me and my family dynamic, probably better than I did. He stood by me and encouraged me to keep living life to its fullest during some of my toughest times in high school. I am so grateful that our lives crossed when they did to help me be strong and know that I was okay as I was. I live this life knowing he has missed so many years that I have been gifted. I dedicate my journey to him and I will never take it for granted.

To my parents and brothers, I acknowledge the journey we have taken together and separately. Although we each may have different perspectives, I honor the fact we are human and trying to make the best way we can in life. Maybe we cannot all be together because of our experiences, but I wish you love and peace in your lives. Hopefully our stories can help others and good can come out of our experiences.

I would like to thank all the people who have contributed to this book in some way, whether through their stories, edits, or reviews. You have helped make my ideas and stories meaningful to readers. Thanks to Matthew Solan, Anjanette Harper, Elizabeth Brown, Sharna Brockett, Stephanie Cable, Mary Jo Huelskamp, Kacee Johnson, Byron Patrick, Bharat Nain, Jennifer Fitzpatrick, Joseph Oniwor, Jeremy Jones, Tye and Samantha Moe, Madeline Pratt, James DeLeo, Scott Shute, Melisa Galasso, James Leath, Bonnie Bennett, and Tracy Mink.

Thanks to all the yoga teachers and mindfulness instructors that I have learned from over the last 16 years. Every single person has left their impact on my journey and the teachings I pass on in my work today.

To everyone that has supported me in the work I do, thank you from my heart that I have the privilege to do the work I do each day. I could not do what I do without you choosing to go on this path with me. I honor the light within you. Namaste.

About the Author

AMY VETTER is an accomplished C-suite executive, prior CPA firm partner, and CEO of multiple accounting practices. She has deep experience in cloud technology and business strategy transformation, as well as being a certified yoga and mindfulness teacher. She combines her business and yoga experience in the books she has authored, *Business, Balance & Bliss: How the B3 Method Can Transform Your Career & Life* and *Integrative Advisory Services: Taking Your Accounting Services Beyond the Cloud*, and the keynote programs she delivers.

Amy is a board member and committee member for multiple organizations. As a CPA CITP, CGMA, Amy is also a key influencer in the accounting and finance profession. She has been named one of the "Most Powerful Women in Accounting" by the AICPA and *CPA Practice Advisor* and a Top 100 Most Influential Person by *Accounting Today* multiple times.

Amy is the podcast host of *Breaking Beliefs* and shares her accounting and business insights as a contributor to AICPA's *Journal of Accountancy, Accounting Today,* and *CPA Practice Advisor* as well as *Inc.com* and *Entrepreneur.com.*

You can find out more about Amy at www.amyvetter.com or follow her on Facebook, Twitter, Instagram, or LinkedIn @amyvettercpa.